PRODUCTION AND COST FUNCTIONS

To the cricket, rugby and soccer fanatics, and all the other staff members, in the department.

Production and Cost Functions
Specification, measurement and applications

Edited by
ERKIN I. BAIRAM
University of Otago

LONDON AND NEW YORK

First published 1998 by Ashgate Publishing

Reissued 2018 by Routledge
2 Park Square, Milton Park, Abingdon, Oxon OX14 4RN
711 Third Avenue, New York, NY 10017, USA

Routledge is an imprint of the Taylor & Francis Group, an informa business

Copyright © Erkin I. Bairam 1998

All rights reserved. No part of this book may be reprinted or reproduced or utilised in any form or by any electronic, mechanical, or other means, now known or hereafter invented, including photocopying and recording, or in any information storage or retrieval system, without permission in writing from the publishers.

Notice:
Product or corporate names may be trademarks or registered trademarks, and are used only for identification and explanation without intent to infringe.

Publisher's Note
The publisher has gone to great lengths to ensure the quality of this reprint but points out that some imperfections in the original copies may be apparent.

Disclaimer
The publisher has made every effort to trace copyright holders and welcomes correspondence from those they have been unable to contact.

A Library of Congress record exists under LC control number: 98071456

ISBN 13: 978-1-138-71629-2 (hbk)
ISBN 13: 978-1-138-71628-5 (pbk)
ISBN 13: 978-1-315-19705-0 (ebk)

Contents

Contributors		vi
Preface		vii
1	The Popular and Some New Non-Homogeneous Production Functions *Erkin I. Bairam*	1
2	Production and Cost Functions: An Accountant's Viewpoint *Roger Willett*	17
3	Production versus Cost Functions: Unreliability of the Duality Theorem in Accounting and Economics *Erkin I. Bairam and Emel Kahya*	42
4	The Box-Cox Transformation as a VES Production Function *Murat Genç and Erkin I. Bairam*	54
5	The Form of Production Function for the Chinese Regional Economy *Erkin I. Bairam*	62
6	Linear versus Non-Linear Technical Progress and Production Functions: Theory and Some Evidence *Erkin I. Bairam*	68
7	The Measurement of Technical Change and the Estimation of Factor Demand *Chris Doucouliagos and Phillip Hone*	82
8	Pass-Through Elasticities for Production Costs and Competing Foreign Prices: Evidence from Manufacturing Prices in Seven Countries *Harry Bloch and Michael Olive*	106
9	Non-Linear Costs and Returns to Scale: Some Disaggregate Results *Erkin I. Bairam*	125

Contributors

Erkin I. Bairam, Department of Economics, University of Otago, PO Box 56, Dunedin, New Zealand; ebairam@commerce.otago.ac.nz

Harry Bloch, Department of Economics, Curtin University of Technology, GPO Box U1987, Perth, Western Australia 6845; BlochH@cbs.curtin.edu.au

Chris Doucouliagos, School of Economics, Deakin University, 221 Burwood Highway, Burwood, Victoria 3125, Australia; douc@deakin.edu.au

Murat Genç, Department of Economics, University of Otago, PO Box 56, Dunedin, New Zealand; mgenc@commerce.otago.ac.nz

Phillip Hone, School of Economics, Deakin University, 221 Burwood Highway, Burwood, Victoria 3125, Australia; hone@deakin.edu.au

Emel Kahya, School of Business, Rutgers University, Camden, New Jersey, USA; kahya@crab.rutgers.edu

Michael Olive, Department of Economics, Curtin University of Technology, GPO Box U1987, Perth, Western Australia 6845.

Roger Willett, School of Accountancy, Faculty of Business, Queensland University of Technology, GPO Box 2434, Brisbane 4001, Australia; r.willett@qut.edu.au

Preface

This book is based on applied and theoretical production and cost papers presented at the 1997 Australasian Meeting of the Econometric Society, at Melbourne University, and articles written by the Editor and his colleagues.

All articles include focus on different aspects of aggregation, specification and interpretation of conventional and new production and cost functions.

Erkin I. Bairam,
Dunedin,
New Zealand,
December 1997

1 The Popular and Some New Non-Homogeneous Production Functions

Erkin I. Bairam

I. INTRODUCTION

In the production literature, it is well known that functions used in applied research are, without *a priori* tests, assumed to be not only homogeneous but linear homogeneous. Unfortunately, it is not generally known that the homogeneity (and hence, the constant scale elasticity) assumption is not appropriate for some aspects of the production theory.

Ringstad (1974) and Bairam (1991b) have shown that much of the theoretical work is based on production functions with a scale elasticity which decreases with increase in output. This contrasts with many popular production functions used in applied studies which assume the same returns to scale at all levels of output.

The following quotation eloquently summarises the main limitations of the homogeneity assumptions:

> Production functions most commonly used in empirical research are homogeneous i.e., they have constant scale elasticity [see section II], like the Cobb-Douglas and CES production functions. On the other hand much of the theoretical work is based on production functions with a scale elasticity which is decreasing when at least one factor is increasing and none is decreasing. The difference between scale elasticities can be illustrated many ways. In Figure 1 we illustrate how the average cost curve may look when we have: i) a homogeneous production function with scale elasticity above one, ii) the same type of production function with a scale elasticity below one, and iii) an inhomogeneous production function with a scale elasticity decreasing from values above one to values below one. (Ringstad (1974, p.88)).

Consequently, as early as 1973, Christensen *et al.* argued that it is important to develop tests of the theory of production that do not employ homogeneity as part of the maintained hypothesis. More recently Fuss *et al.* (1978) went even further and emphasised that flexible functional forms, embodying few maintained hypotheses, should be used to test fundamental hypotheses of the production theory. Given this background, it is important to examine such new and not-so-new production functions in some detail and this will be the main objective of this paper.

Consequently, in this chapter new non-homogeneous functions by the present author, as well as, the popular non-homogeneous production functions developed in the late 1960's and early 1970's are examined and discussed. In section II important properties of the neo-classical production function, which are relevant for the discussion here, are briefly discussed. In section III, the new non-homogeneous CES production function is examined and its estimation procedures are discussed. Section IV examines variable elasticity of substitution production functions (VES) which are also variable scale elasticity (i.e. non-homogeneous) functions. In this section appropriate econometric estimation procedures that can be used to obtain parameters of these functions are also discussed. Finally, section V concludes the chapter.

II. THE NEO-CLASSICAL PRODUCTION FUNCTION

The conventional production function theory begins with two inputs (labour, L, and capital, K) which are combined to produce a unique maximum quantity of output (Q):

$$Q = f(L, K) \qquad (1)$$

The function f defines the technical relationship between the two inputs and output. It is assumed to be continuous and, at least, twice differentiable.

The neo-classical production function requires that marginal products of labour (f_L) and capital (f_K) are positive and decreasing. That is writing $(\partial Q/\partial L) = f_L$; $(\partial^2 Q/\partial L^2) = f_{LL}$ and so forth, the production function assumes:

$$f_L > 0; \; f_K > 0; \; f_{LL} < 0: \; f_{KK} < 0 \qquad (2)$$

The neo-classical production function is also assumed to be homogeneous (see, *inter alia*, Chambers (1988) and Bairam (1991b)). That is to say if labour and capital are increased by some proportion h, then Q may increase in the same proportion, or by some larger or smaller proportion, namely:

$$f(hL, hK) = h^\upsilon (L, K) = h^\upsilon Q \qquad (3)$$

υ, therefore, gives the degree of homogeneity of the function f. A value of $\upsilon = 1$ indicates constant returns to scale and increasing or decreasing returns to scale are given by values of υ greater or less than unity. A homogeneous production function always yields a total scale elasticity, ε, which is *constant* and equal to υ.[1] Another important property of homogeneous functions is given by Euler's theorem, which says that the sum of the first partial derivatives weighted by the quantity of the factor inputs is equal to output times the degree of homogeneity:

$$f_L L + f_K K = \upsilon Q \qquad (4)$$

In the case of linear homogeneous production functions ($\upsilon = 1$), this clearly suggests that if factors are paid their marginal product there will be no profits or losses — which suggests perfect competition.[2]

Turning to another parameter of interest in a production function, namely, the marginal rate of technical substitution, M, and the elasticity of substitution, σ, will be extensively used in this paper. The marginal rate of technical substitution is given by:

$$M = -(\partial K/\partial L) = (f_L/f_K) \qquad (5)$$

is positive, as $f_L, f_K > 0$; it is also assumed to decrease as substitution proceeds — given that an isoquant is convex to the origin (equation (2)).

The elasticity of substitution, σ, the other parameter of interest can be derived using (5). It is defined as the proportionate change in factor input ratio as a result of a proportionate change in the marginal rate of technical substitution, arithmetically:

$$\sigma = [d\log(K/L)/d\log M] \qquad (6)$$

It is clear that this parameter is always non-negative and it measures the ease of substitution between labour and capital. As it will be shown, in

---

[1] Before going any further, it is worthwhile to define total scale elasticity. Total scale elasticity is the sum of the output elasticities, ε_i, namely: $\varepsilon = \Sigma \varepsilon_i = \Sigma[(\partial Q/\partial X_i)(X_i/Q_i)]$ where X_i is input i and Q is, as before, the output level.

[2] An important property of the linear homogeneous production function is that, it can be written, in per capita terms, as a function of one variable which makes it very attractive in applied work. That is to say, setting $h = 1/L$ equation (3) becomes:
$(Q/L) = f(K/L, 1)$ where (Q/L) is the level of output productivity (output per capita) and (K/L) is the capital-labour ratio.

section III and IV, it can be constant or variable, depending upon the production function (i.e. f) under consideration.

III. THE NEW NON-HOMOGENEOUS CES PRODUCTION FUNCTION

The new CES function, unlike the Arrow et al. (1961) and other CES functions used in the literature, is *not* homogeneous. It has been introduced by the present author (Bairam (1989, 1991a, 1991b), Bairam et al. (1990) and see also Bairam and Dasgupta (1993) and Hsing (1993)). It is specified as a general Box-Cox (1964) model:

$$[(Q^\lambda - 1)/\lambda] = A(t) + \alpha [(L^\lambda - 1)/\lambda] + \beta [(K^\lambda - 1)/\lambda] \qquad (7)$$

where $\lambda \leq 1$ and $A(t), \alpha, \beta > 0$.

This function includes, as a special case, the popular Cobb-Douglas, since when $\lambda = 0$ (7) is reduced to:[3]

$$\ln Q = A(t) + \alpha \ln L + \beta \ln K \qquad (8)$$

and, therefore, $\varepsilon = \upsilon = \alpha + \beta$ (see below).

This production function in (7) has the following marginal productivity properties:

$$f_L = \alpha (L/Q)^{\lambda - 1} \qquad (9)$$

$$f_K = \beta (K/Q)^{\lambda - 1} \qquad (10)$$

and

$$f_{LL} = \alpha (L/Q)^{\lambda - 1} L^{-1} (1-\lambda) [\alpha (L/Q)^\lambda - 1] \qquad (11)$$

$$f_{KK} = \beta (K/Q)^{\lambda - 1} K^{-1} (1-\lambda) (\beta (K/Q)^\lambda - 1) \qquad (12)$$

Therefore, it is clear from (9) and (10) that the marginal products of labour and capital are positive. Furthermore, as long as $\lambda < 1$ and $\alpha(L/Q)^\lambda > 1$, $\beta(K/Q)^\lambda > 1$, equation (7) satisfies the second order requirements of the neo-classical production function (see section 2).

Turning to elasticity of substitution (equation (6), since marginal rate of technical substitution (equation (5)) is given by:

---

[3] That is because using the Taylor series for expansion, it can be shown that when $\lambda \to 0$, $[(X^\lambda - 1)/\lambda] \approx \ln X$, where $X = Q$, L or K.

$$M = (\alpha/\beta)(L/K)^{\lambda-1} \qquad (13)$$

the elasticity of substitution for this production function is:

$$\sigma = (1-\lambda)^{-1} \qquad (14)$$

and, hence, it is clear from (14) that:

and
$$\sigma \geq 0 \quad \text{as} \quad \lambda \leq 1$$
$$\sigma < 0 \quad \text{as} \quad \lambda > 1$$

Thus, as long as the functional form is restricted to values of lambda no greater than unity, equation (7) is a CES production function. It is clear that in this model the elasticity of substitution depends upon the value of lambda obtained from the data used for estimation purposes. For example, if the estimated lambda is equal to zero, then σ is equal to unity — i.e. the Cobb-Douglas production function (equation (8)) is the correct model.

Finally, turning to another parameter of interest, namely the total scale elasticity, ε (see, footnote 1), for the new CES production function discussed here, it is given by:

$$\varepsilon = \alpha(Q/L)^{-\lambda} + (Q/K)^{-\lambda} \qquad (15)$$

Therefore, since (7) is non-homogeneous, as expected, the scale elasticity is variable and depends upon the labour and capital productivity levels which are not constants. It is also clear from (15) that $(\partial \varepsilon/\partial Z) \gtreqless 0$, where $Z = (Q/L)$ or $Z = (Q/K)$, as $\lambda \gtreqless 0$; for $\lambda < 0$ ($\sigma < 1$) ε increases as labour and capital productivities increase, while for $1 > \lambda > 0$ ($\sigma > 1$) ε decreases as the productivities increase. Moreover, it is also clear that for $\lambda = 0$ (the Cobb-Douglas, equation (8)), the function is homogeneous and the degree of homogeneity is $\varepsilon = \alpha + \beta$ and, hence, $(\partial \varepsilon/\partial Z) = 0$.

Last but not least, since this new CES function is being used in applied research it is important to discuss the procedures that can be used for estimation purposes.

Taking equation (7) and adding an error term, e, to it gives the specification used for estimation purposes. To estimate such a equation using maximum-likelihood, it is generally assumed that the error term is normally distributed. Unfortunately, the Box-Cox transformation approach implies that the distribution of e is truncated, and, therefore, it cannot be normally distributed (see, for example, Fomby et al. (1984) and Judge et al. (1985)). To proceed with maximum likelihood estimation, the present author assumes that truncation effects are negligible and the e's are approximately independently identically distributed random variables with zero mean and constant variance. Under this assumption the joint probability density function for $\mathbf{e} = (e_1, e_2, e_3, ..., e_4)'$ is given by:

$$f(\mathbf{e}) = (2\pi\sigma^2)^{-n/2} \text{ ext } (-\mathbf{e}'\mathbf{e}/2\sigma^2) \qquad (16)$$

To write the joint pdf for $\mathbf{Q} = (Q_1, Q_2, Q_3, ..., Q_n)'$, given the parameters and explanatory variables (L and K) the Jacobian of the transformation of $\mathbf{e}$ to $\mathbf{Q}$ is required. Since, $(\partial \mathbf{Q}/\partial \mathbf{e}) = \mathbf{Q}^{\lambda-1}$ and $\mathbf{J} = \Pi(|\partial \mathbf{e}/\partial \mathbf{Q}|)$:

$$\mathbf{J} = \Pi \mathbf{Q}^{\lambda-1} \qquad (17)$$

and the joint pdf for $\mathbf{Q}$ is given by:

$$f(\mathbf{Q}) = (2\pi\sigma^2)^{-n/2} \exp(-\mathbf{e}\mathbf{e}/2\sigma^2) \mathbf{J} \qquad (18)$$

The expression in (18) is viewed as the function of the parameters of the likelihood function, $L(...)$, taking the log of this likelihood function and using (17), (18) can be rewritten as:

$$\ln L = \text{const.} - (n/2)\ln\sigma^2 - 0.5 \sigma^2 \mathbf{e}'\mathbf{e} + (\lambda-1) \Sigma \ln Q \qquad (19)$$

and since $\sigma^2 = (\mathbf{e}'\mathbf{e}/n)$, equation (19) can be respecified as the following concentrated log likelihood function:

$$\ln L = \text{const} - (n/2) \ln\sigma^2 + (\lambda-1)\Sigma \ln Q \qquad (20)$$

Equation (20) can be maximized using the relevant procedures in many econometric computer programs such as Shazam (White (1978)).

IV. VARIABLE SCALE ELASTICITY AND ELASTICITY OF SUBSTITUTION PRODUCTION FUNCTIONS

i) The 'double transformation' production function

In a recent issue of *Applied Economics*, Grimes (1991) commented that the present author's specification of the CES production function, discussed in the previous section, "fails to meet a principal criterion [homogeneity] to be considered a neo-classical production function". However, as emphasized in the introduction, the homogeneity assumption is not even an appropriate one for some aspects of the production theory. In the present author's reply to Grimes (Bairam

(1991b)), it is argued that the problem with the production function under consideration in section 3 was not the homogeneity issue emphasised by Grimes but the assumption of *constant* elasticity of substitution. There, it is shown that this assumption can also be explicitly tested if the following 'double transformation' production function is used:

$$[(((Q^\lambda-1)/\lambda)^\phi-1)/\phi] = A(t) + [(((L^\lambda-1)/\lambda)^\phi-1)/\phi] + \beta[(((K^\lambda-1)/\lambda)^\phi-1)/\phi] \quad (21)$$

where $\lambda < 1$, $\infty^+ > \phi > \infty^-$ and $A(t)$, α, $\beta > 0$.

This production function has the following marginal products:

$$f_L = \alpha[(Q^\lambda-1)/(L^\lambda-1)]^{1-\phi} (Q/L)^{1-\lambda} \quad (22)$$

and

$$f_K = \beta[(Q^\lambda-1)/(L^\lambda-1)]^{1-\phi} (Q/K)^{1-\lambda} \quad (23)$$

Therefore, it is clear from equations (22) and (23) that the marginal products of labour and capital are positive.

Turning next to the parameter of interest, the elasticity of substitution, σ, using the marginal rate of technical substitution (equation (5)) which is given by:

$$M = (\alpha/\beta) [(K^\lambda-1)/(L^\lambda-1)]^{1-\phi} (K/L)^{1-\lambda} \quad (24)$$

yields the elasticity of substitution (equation (6)) as:

$$\sigma = [d\log(K/L)] / \{(1-\phi)d\log[(K^\lambda-1)/(L^\lambda-1)] + (1-\lambda)d\log(K/L)\} \quad (25)$$

It is clear from (25) that providing $\phi \neq 1$ and $\lambda \neq 0$, σ varies along an isoquant, and capital deepening forces σ away from unity. It is also worthwhile to note that if $\phi = 1$, as it can be seen from (25), this VES production function is reduced to the CES production function discussed in section 3 and if $\lambda = 0$ to the homogeneous Cobb-Douglas. Finally, it is important to emphasise that, for any given parameter set, σ is strictly monotonic in (K/L) along an isoquant and equation (21) is not homogeneous unless $\lambda = 0$.

Therefore, summing it up, in this production function the elasticity of substitution depends upon the functional form implied by the data used for estimation purposes and the capital-labour ratio.

This new VES production function is non-linear in parameters and, unfortunately, it is difficult to estimate it directly, even with conventional maximum likelihood procedures. However if the simple economic model is used, and perfect competition in all markets is assumed, important parameters can be estimated from relevant marginal productivity conditions $(w/p) = f_L$ and $(r/p) = f_K$ where (w/p) and (r/p) are the real wage and interest rates, respectively).

Thus, using these marginal productivity conditions and taking the natural logs of equations (22) and (23) give:

$$\ln(w/p) = \ln\alpha + (1-\phi)\ln[(Q^\lambda-1)/(L^\lambda-1)] + (1-\lambda)\ln(Q/L) \qquad (26)$$

and

$$\ln(r/p) = \ln\beta + (1-\phi)\ln[(Q^\lambda-1)/(K^\lambda-1)] + (1-\lambda)\ln(Q/K) \qquad (27)$$

Equations (26) and (27) are still non-linear in λ parameter, but unlike (21), are relatively easy to estimate using conventional maximum-likelihood procedures. The values of λ and ϕ obtained from (26) and/or (27) can be used in (25) to compute the elasticity of substitution.

It is worthwhile to note that Chapter 4 will also demonstrate the extended Box-Cox model with different transformations of the variables which can be interpreted as a VES production function.

ii) The transcendental logarithmic production function

The translog production function introduced by Christensen *et al.* (1971 and 1973) constitutes an important development in the theory of production and its applications. For the two factor case it can be written as:

$$\ln Q = A(t) + \alpha_L \ln L + \alpha_K \ln K + 0.5\alpha_{LL}(\ln L)^2 + \\ 0.5\alpha_{KK}(\ln K)^2 + \alpha_{LK}(\ln L \ln K) \qquad (28)$$

It is clear that in this general form the translog function is not homogeneous and, hence, the scale elasticities of labour and capital vary over time. If capital's elasticity grows relative to that of labour, the increasing weight given to capital, the faster growing input, would cause the index of factor inputs to rise more rapidly and the index of multi-factor productivity to rise more slowly than that with constant elasticities. Alternatively, a growing labour elasticity would cause the productivity to rise more rapidly than that with constant Cobb-Douglas elasticities.

It can be seen from (28) that linear homogeneity (constant returns to scale) requires the following restrictions on the parameters of the production function:

$$\alpha_L + \alpha_K = 1$$
$$\alpha_{LL} + \alpha_{LK} = 0$$
$$\alpha_{KK} + \alpha_{LK} = 0$$

Substituting these restrictions into (28) gives:

$$\ln(Q/L) = A(t) + \alpha_K \ln(K/L) + 0.5\alpha_{KK}[\ln(L/K)]^2 \qquad (29)$$

This is the intensive form of the translog function. It can be seen from (29) that with two factors and constant returns to scale, the translog function simplifies to the conventional CES case.[4] Furthermore, if $\alpha_{KK} = 0$, equation (29) simplifies to linear homogeneous Cobb-Douglas form. In order to allow for tests of the constant returns to scale assumption, as well as the Cobb-Douglas and conventional CES assumptions, equation (28) should be used as the functional form for estimation, and not equation (29), and these restrictions listed above should be *explicitly* tested.

Estimates of the coefficients in equation (28) also allows researchers to compute output elasticities of labour and capital, ε_L and ε_K, from the following expressions:

$$\varepsilon_L = \alpha_L + \alpha_{LL} \ln L + \alpha_{LK} \ln K \qquad (30)$$

and

$$\varepsilon_K = \alpha_K + \alpha_{KK} \ln K + \alpha_{LK} \ln L \qquad (31)$$

Thus, the sum of (30) and (31) yields the total scale elasticity (see footnote 1), namely:

$$\varepsilon = \alpha_L + \alpha_K + (\alpha_{LL} + \alpha_{LK})\ln L + (\alpha_{KK} + \alpha_{LK})\ln K \qquad (32)$$

which in the Cobb-Douglas case, where $\alpha_{LL} = \alpha_{LK} = \alpha_{KK} = 0$, is equal to $\alpha_L + \alpha_K$ and, as expected, is constant.

Unfortunately, although the translog function has been widely used in empirical analysis, until very recently, the intensive linear homogeneous form (equation (29)), and not the general unrestricted form (equation (28)), is used in applied work.[5] Kim (1992) has argued that this is mainly because "... most of the existing estimation methods are valid for homogeneous production functions with fixed scale effects" (p.552). His paper has provided a new framework to estimate a non-homogeneous translog production function that allows for variable returns to scale. Kim's results for USA manufacturing reveal that neither homogeneity nor constant returns to scale is a proper description of the underlying USA production technology. Consequently, he argues that this calls into question all earlier

---
[4] This can be seen by comparing (29) with the Kmenta (1967) approximation of the CES.
[5] See, for example, Berndt and Christensen (1973), Berndt (1976) Carbo and Meller (1979) and the brief review and the references in Chung (1987).

production analysis that impose homogeneity in general, and constant returns to scale in particular.

Lastly, it is important to show that the elasticity of substitution for the unrestricted version of translog. The elasticity of substitution can be defined as:

$$\sigma = (\varepsilon/Q)[\varepsilon - \alpha_{LL}(\varepsilon_K/\varepsilon_L) - \alpha_{KK}(\varepsilon_L/\varepsilon_K) - 2\alpha_{LK}]^{-1} \quad (33)$$

where ε_L, ε_K and $\varepsilon = \varepsilon_L + \varepsilon_K$ are defined above in equations (30), (31) and (32). Hence, the elasticity of substitution for translog depends upon variables Q, L and K. Thus, as expected, σ is variable.

iii) The constant marginal share production function

In his study of factor contribution to growth in the Israeli economy, where neither the labour nor the capital market could be assumed to be in equilibrium, Bruno (1968) introduced the following VES production function:

$$Q = A(t) L^\alpha K^\beta - \gamma L \quad (34)$$

where $A(t) > 0$ and $1 > \alpha, \beta > 0$

As the name suggests, this is a constant marginal share (CMS) production function and has the following neo-classical properties:

$$f_L = \alpha A(t) L^{\alpha-1} K^\beta - \gamma > 0 \text{ if } (...) > \gamma \text{ or } \gamma < 0 \quad (35)$$

$$f_K = \beta A(t) L^\alpha K^{\beta-1} > 0 \quad (36)$$

$$f_{LL} = \alpha (\alpha - 1) A(t) L^{\alpha-2} K^\beta < 0 \quad (37)$$

$$f_{KK} = \beta (\beta - 1) A(t) L^\alpha K^{\beta-2} < 0 \quad (38)$$

That is to say, it is clear from equations (35) - (38) that marginal products of labour and capital (f_L and f_K) are positive but they increase at a decreasing rate.

The scale elasticities of labour and capital are given by:

$$\begin{aligned}\varepsilon_L = f_L(L/Q) &= (\alpha A(t) L^{\alpha-1}K^\beta - \gamma)(L/Q) \\ &= (\alpha A(t) L^\alpha K^\beta - \gamma L) Q^{-1} \\ &= \alpha \end{aligned} \quad (39)$$

and

$$\varepsilon_K = f_K(K/Q) = (\beta\, A(t)\, L^\alpha K^{\beta-1})\,(K/Q)$$
$$= (\beta\, A(t)\, L^\alpha K^\beta)\, Q^{-1} \qquad (40)$$

The sum of (38) and (39) gives the total scale elasticity (see, footnote 1):

$$\varepsilon = \varepsilon_L + \varepsilon_K = \alpha + [(\beta\, A(t)\, L^\alpha K^\beta)\, Q^{-1}]$$
$$= \alpha + [\beta\,(Q + \gamma L)\, Q^{-1}]$$
$$= \alpha + \beta + [\beta\gamma(L/Q)] \qquad (41)$$

It is obvious from (41), not withstanding the fact that the labour scale elasticities are constant, because the capital scale elasticity is variable, the total scale elasticity is variable. The elasticity of substitution implied by this VES production is given by the following expression:

$$\sigma = 1 - [(\beta\gamma)/\alpha]\,(L/Q) \qquad (42)$$

When $0 < \beta < 1$, (42) has the following properties: when $\gamma > 0$, the elasticity of substitution is always less than 1 and monotonically approaches 1 from below, as Q increases. Similarly, when $\gamma < 0$, the elasticity of substitution is always greater than 1 and monotonically approaches 1 from above, as Q increases. This could also be seen from direct inspection of the form of the production function (34). It is clear that when $\gamma = 0$, equation (34) collapses to the Cobb-Douglas production function and, not surprisingly from (42), it is clear that $\sigma = 1$.

Finally it is worthwhile to note that since the shift factor $A(t)$ multiplies only the first-term of the production function (i.e. the Cobb-Douglas component), technical progress will be neutral only asymptotically, as t becomes large. Otherwise, its effect is to increase or decrease, the marginal rate of technical substitution, M (equation (5)) for any given (K/L), according to whether γ is positive or negative. The case $\gamma > 0$ in which technical progress starts off being 'capital saving' (M increases with t) is interesting. One way of looking at this might be that of the labour force undergoing some process of 'learning' with time in a way that increases their marginal product in relation to that of capital (Arrow (1962)). This may very well be a more realistic description for an economy in early stages of rapid industrialisation than the ordinary 'neutrality' assumption (i.e. $\gamma = 0$).

Turning to the estimation of the CMS function, equation (34) can be estimated by non-linear procedures such as maximum likelihood and non-linear least squares. It should also be noted that when $\alpha + \beta = 1$

(i.e. when $\gamma = 0$ also, constant returns to scale), equation (34) can be rewritten as:

$$(Q/L) = A(t) (K/L)^{\beta - \gamma} \tag{43}$$

However, a direct non-linear estimation procedure still must be used to obtain non-linear confidence intervals for the parameters.

iv) **A simple multiplicative non-homogeneous production function**

A log-linear production function is recently specified by Bairam (1992) as:

$$Q = A(t) L^{\alpha_1 + \beta_1 \ln K} K^{\alpha_2 + \beta_2 \ln L} \tag{44}$$

where $A(t)$, $\alpha_1, \alpha_2 > 0$ and $\beta_1, \beta_2 \gtrless 0$

This production function has the following theoretical properties:

$$(\partial \ln Q/\partial \ln L) = \varepsilon_L = \alpha_1 + (\beta_1 + \beta_2)\ln K \tag{45}$$

$$(\partial \ln Q/\partial \ln K) = \varepsilon_K = \alpha_2 + (\beta_1 + \beta_2)\ln L \tag{46}$$

Therefore given these output elasticities of labour and capital, the total scale elasticity is (see footnote 1):

$$\varepsilon = \varepsilon_L + \varepsilon_K = \alpha_1 + \alpha_2 + (\beta_1 + \beta_2)\ln(LK) \tag{47}$$

which is variable.

Differentiating equation (44) with respect to L and K yields the marginal products of labour and capital, respectively, which are:

$$f_L = (Q/L)\varepsilon_L \tag{48}$$

and

$$f_K = (Q/K)\varepsilon_K \tag{49}$$

Therefore, the marginal products can be negative, if and only if ε_i, $i = L, K$, are negative. Hence, $[-\alpha_1 < (\beta_1 + \beta_2)\ln K]$ and $[-\alpha_2 < (\beta_1 + \beta_2)\ln L]$ have to be satisfied to have both marginal products positive.

Another parameter of interest, namely, the elasticity of substitution between labour and capital, is given by:

$$\begin{aligned}\sigma &= (\varepsilon_L + \varepsilon_K)\,[\varepsilon_L + \varepsilon_K + 2(\beta_1 + \beta_2)]^{-1} \\ &= [\alpha_1 + \alpha_2 + (\beta_1 + \beta_2)\ln(LK)]^{-1} \\ &= \{\alpha_1 + \alpha_2 + (\beta_1 + \beta_2)[2 + \ln(LK)]\}^{-1}\end{aligned} \qquad (50)$$

It is clear that in this model the elasticity of substitution is variable, as it does not just depend upon constant parameters but upon the variable (lnL + lnK), as well. It is worthwhile to emphasise that if $\beta_1 = \beta_2 = 0$, this VES function is reduced to the Cobb-Douglas production function and if $\beta_2 = 0$, it is equivalent to the Vinod (1972) function.

Finally, turning to the estimation of this non-linear production function, it can be estimated using maximum likelihood or non-linear least squares. Another way of estimating it, however, is to linearise it. Taking logs of equation (43) and re-arranging it, gives:

$$\ln Q = \ln A(t) + \alpha_1 \ln L + \alpha_2 \ln K + \beta \ln(LK) \qquad (51)$$

where $\beta = \beta_1 + \beta_2$.

This log-linear model can be estimated using ordinary least squares. Therefore, this specification is easier than (43) to estimate and, in terms of compilation of costs much cheaper. However, it has one limitation: it yields the reduced form parameter β, hence, the structural parameters β_1 and β_2 cannot be computed separately.

v) A simple additive non-homogeneous production function

Sudit (1973) suggested the following additive non-homogeneous production function:

$$Q = A(t) + \alpha_1 L + \beta_1 K + \alpha_2 L \ln K + \beta_2 K \ln L \qquad (52)$$

This function yields the following marginal productivities:

$$f_L = \alpha_1 + \alpha_2 \ln K + \beta_2 (K/L) \qquad (53)$$

and

$$f_K = \beta_1 + \beta_2 \ln L + \alpha_2 (L/K) \qquad (54)$$

It is clear that, as long as α_1, α_2, β_1 and β_2 are positive, the marginal products are positive, furthermore (52) exhibits diminishing returns with respect to both inputs as:

$$f_{LL} = -\beta_2 (K/L) \qquad (55)$$

and

$$f_{KK} = -\alpha_2 (L/K) \qquad (56)$$

However, if α_2 and/or β_2 are negative, one or both inputs could well exhibit increasing returns to the factor. The scale elasticity, which is given by the sum of the marginal elasticities, is given by:

$$\varepsilon = \varepsilon_L + \varepsilon_K = Q^{-1} (f_L L + f_K K)$$
$$= 1 + [Q^{-1} (\alpha_2 L + \beta_2 K)] \quad (57)$$

Hence, since (52) is not homogeneous, the scale elasticity is variable and it can assume any value. The conditions $\alpha_2 \gtreqless$ and $\beta_2 \gtreqless 0$ assure $\varepsilon \gtreqless 1$. It is also clear from (56) that if $\alpha_2 = \beta_2 = 0$, then $\varepsilon = 1$, that is to say constant returns to scale prevail and, as it can be seen from (52), the production is reduced to the linearly homogeneous additive formulation: $Q = A(t) + \alpha_1 L + \alpha_2 K$.

Last but not least, from (52), it can also be shown that this non-homogeneous production function is also a variable elasticity of substitution function. The elasticity of substitution could be numerically computed by the well know expression:

$$\sigma = [(f_L + f_K)(f_L L + f_K K)][(-LK)(f_{LL} f_K{}^2 - 2 f_{LK} f_L f_K + f_{KK} f_L{}^2)]^{-1} \quad (58)$$

V. CONCLUSION

The objective of this article has been to discuss specification and estimation of different production functions which do not impose the assumption of homogeneity as part of the maintained hypothesis. Three of the functions examined are new (the non-homogeneous CES, the double transformation and simple multiplicative production functions) and the other three are well established, relatively popular ones (the translog, the CMS and simple additive production functions).

All of these functions contrast with many current popular production functions used in applied studies (e.g. the Cobb-Douglas and the conventional CES) which assume the same returns to scale to all levels of output (i.e. homogeneity). The production functions presented here exhibit scale elasticities which vary with the scale of operations and have a elasticity of substitution which is constant (section III) or variable (section IV).

As long ago as 1932, Hicks in his *The Theory of Wages* noted that in the absence of technological change an increasing capital-labour ratio might induce a tendency towards a diminishing elasticity of substitution, thereby at least implicitly recognizing the possibility of the variable elasticity of substitution. This statement seems to have gone largely overlooked until the early 1970's when the translog was introduced. Here, in section IV, the non-homogeneous production functions analysed are also VES. It is hoped that from now on they will enjoy more popularity than in the past, and will be subjected to more empirical testing.

Last but not least, it is worthwhile to note that most functions discussed here, possess the same limitations as many other production functions. First it is difficult to generalise as most of these functions include more than two inputs. Second, the two Box-Cox functions and the CMS function are non-linear in parameters and, therefore, are relatively difficult to estimate.

REFERENCES

Arrow, K.J. (1962), The Economic implications of learning-by-doing, *Review of Economic Studies*, 29, pp. 225-250.

Arrow, K.J., Chenery, H.B., Minhas, R.S. and Solow, R.M. (1961), Capital-labour substitution and economic efficiency, *Review of Economics and Statistics*, 43, pp. 225-250.

Bairam, E.I. (1989), Functional form and the elasticity of substitution: a new CES production function, *Economics Discussion Papers*, No. 8904, University of Otago, New Zealand.

Bairam, E.I. (1991a), Elasticity of substitution, technical progress and returns to scale in branches of Soviet industry: a new CES production function approach. *Journal of Applied Econometrics*, 6, pp. 91-96.

Bairam, E.I. (1991b), Functional form and new production functions: some comments and a new VES function, *Applied Economics*, 23, pp. 1247-1250.

Bairam, E.I. (1992), A log-linear non-homogeneous production function: specification and estimation, *Economics Discussion Papers*, No. 9218, University of Otago, New Zealand.

Bairam, E.I. and Dasgupta, A.K. (1993), The elasticity of substitution and its effects on the wage rate in manufacturing branches of Indian industry, in E.I. Bairam (ed), *Studies in labour economics*, Avebury, Aldershot.

Bairam, E.I., Howells, J.M. and Turner, G.M. (1990), Production function in cricket: the Australian and New Zealand experience, *Applied Economics*, 22, pp. 871-879.

Berndt, E.R. (1976), Reconciling alternative estimates of the elasticity of substitution, *Review of Economics and Statistics*, 58, pp. 59-68.

Berndt, E.R. and Christensen, L.R. (1973), The translog function and the substitution of equipment, structures and labour in U.S. manufacturing, 1929-68, *Journal of Econometrics*, 1, pp. 81-113.

Box, G.E.P. and Cox, D.P. (1964), An analysis of transformations, *Journal of Royal Statistical Society*, Series B, 26, pp. 211-252.

Bruno, M. (1968), Estimation of factor contributions to growth under structural disequilibrium, *International Economic Review*, 9, pp. 49-62.

Carbo, V. and Meller, P. (1979), The translog production function: some evidence from establishment data, *Journal of Econometrics*, 10, pp. 193-199.

Christensen, L.R., Jorgensen, D.W. and Lau, L.J. (1971), Conjugate, duality and the transcedental logarithmic production function, *Econometrica*, 39, pp. 225-256.

Christensen, L.R., Jorgensen, D.W. and Lau, L.J. (1973), Transcendental logarithmic production frontiers, *Review of Economics and Statistics*, 55, pp. 28-45.

Chung, J.W. (1987), On the estimation for factor substitution in the translog model, *Review of Economics and Statistics*, 69, pp. 409-417.

Fomby, T.B., Hill, R.C.and Johnson, S.R. (1984), *Advanced econometric methods*, Springer-Verlag, New York.

Fuss, M., McFadden, D.and Mundalak, Y. (1978), A survey of functional forms in economic analysis of production, in M. Fuss and D. McFadden (eds), *Production economics, Vol. 1, The theory of production*, North-Holland, Amsterdam.

Grimes, A. (1991), A new production function? Bowled by a googly?, *Applied Economics*, 23, pp. 1245-1246.

Hicks, J.R. (1932), *The theory of wages*, Macmillan, London.

Hsing, Y. (1993), The choice of production functions: the case of US manufacturing industries, *Applied Economics*, 25, pp. 321-324.

Judge, G.G., Griffiths, W.E., Hill, R.C., Luthkepohl, H. and Lee, T.C. (1985), *The theory and practice of econometrics*, 2nd edition, Wiley, New York.

Kim, Y.H. (1992), The translog production function and variable returns to scale, *Review of Economics and Statistics*, 74, pp. 546-552.

Kmenta, J. (1967), On estimation of the CES production function, *International Economic Review*, 8, pp. 180-189.

Ringstad, V. (1974), Some empirical evidence on the decreasing scale elasticity, *Econometrica*, 42, pp. 87-101.

Sudit, E.F. (1973), Additive non-homogeneous production functions in telecommunications, *Bell Journal of Economics and Management Science*, 4, pp. 499-514.

Vinod, H.D. (1972), Non-homogeneous production functions and applications to telecommunications, *Bell Journal of Economics and Management Science*, 3, pp. 531-543.

White, K.J. (1978), A general computer program for econometric methods - Shazam, *Econometrica*, 46, pp. 239-240.

2 Production and Cost Functions: An Accountant's Viewpoint

Roger Willett

I. INTRODUCTION

The theory of production functions is taught to many aspiring accountants for the first time in courses in economics. For the student without practical experience in preparing financial statements the conceptual apparatus that is learnt typically turns out later to be unhelpful or misleading in actual measurement situations. For the student with some practical background in accounting the concepts, while having some intuitive plausibility, usually seem remote from experience. This essay discusses the reasons for this state of affairs and considers in some detail an alternative general theory of production functions from an 'accountant's' viewpoint. Although informally termed as such, this reference to the accountant's viewpoint should not be taken to imply that accountants have a different 'world view' from economists or that the subject matter that they measure is different from that studied in economic theory. The alternative is offered as a more general and operational approach to understanding the properties of production functions. This endeavour is motivated by a desire to more clearly base theoretical constructs upon measurable accounting variables thereby allowing the development of properly testable economic theories.

This chapter considers the accounting problems of describing and measuring production, cost and profit functions in practice and the implications of this for economic theory and the econometric estimation of these functions and other related matters. Many economists and econometricians tend to interpret the financial data provided by accountants from the viewpoint of neo-classical economic theory. Due to the difficulties associated with operationalising this theoretical approach significant problems arise in econometric work in comparing facts with theories. An alternative approach to understanding the nature and properties of production, cost and profit functions based upon accounting measurements is outlined in this chapter. Basic concepts are defined at the most micro-economic level in terms of observable (and measurable) variables. It is shown how this characterization supports a general statistical understanding of production, cost and profit functions and how it relates to the problem of aggregation.

II. PRODUCTION AND COST FUNCTIONS IN ECONOMIC THEORY

The term 'production function' in economic theory is usually associated with the description of hypothetical physical input-output relationships, i.e. the variables described by the particular theory are expressed in non-financial measurements. The general functional specification is

$$O = f(I_i), i = 1 \text{ to } n \qquad (1)$$

where O is a physical output measure and the I_i are physical input measures.[6] In theoretical analysis the inputs are often restricted to two different kinds, denoted L and K to stand for 'labour' and 'capital' respectively. An example of one such theory is the so-called 'Cobb-Douglas' production function,

$$O = A(t)L^\alpha K^\beta \qquad (2)$$

Here $A(t)$ is a time dependent 'scale parameter' which supposedly denotes a technological progress variable and α and β are further parameters affecting the shape of the relationship between the dependent and independent variables.[7] Many other specific forms of production functions have been discussed theoretically and examined econometrically. These include 'homogeneous' functions like the Cobb-Douglas (which share the property that, for any proportionate change in inputs, output changes by that same proportion raised to some power) and others where the assumption of homogeneity is relaxed (see Bairam, 1994 and Chapter 1). With the exception of the Linear Programming interpretation of production functions, little thought appears to have been given to the basic measurement question of whether mathematical expressions such as that described in (2) actually do map real empirical properties into the number system.

Some reservations about the representational faithfulness of production functions of the form of (2) were raised in the 'capital theory' debate of the 1960s and 1970s. Robinson (1956) and Sraffa

---

[6] This is a technical, engineering relationship and in applied economic research, in practice, what is used is the value version in which O is replaced by the value of output and the Is are replaced by the values of the inputs.

[7] In the case of the Cobb-Douglas production function α represents the 'elasticity of output due to labour' and β the 'elasticity of output due to capital'.

(1960) criticized and struggled with the notion that 'capital' might be valued in units independent of prices. Neo-classicists such as Solow (1957), Samuelson (1962) and Fisher (1969) tried in various ways to justify the use of the physical aggregate production function in theoretical and applied research. Sraffa demonstrated the difficulties involved in attempting to construct a unique, physical unit of measurement for capital even in the rigid, classical framework of fixed factor output proportions and output mix. Samuelson, at a level of analysis closer to that at which accounting measurement actually takes place, attempted to show that simple, heterogeneous production functions, when combined together, might give the appearance of behaving like the aggregate production function of neo-classical economic theory. However, this was carried through on the basis of a long list of assumptions, which would seem inexplicable to accountants lacking a background in economic theory (e.g. perfect knowledge and perfect competition).

The accountant, alas, is forced to construct measurements in the real world where the assumptions made in economic theory evidently do not often (and perhaps never) hold. Were accounting measurements based upon such assumptions it would therefore, save in exceptional circumstances, not be possible to interpret them.[8] This would be a truly regrettable state of affairs given the fact that accounting numbers are overwhelmingly the source of information upon which business decisions are made (and thus by which the behaviour of the variables of the economic system are determined). Econometricians usually have to work with data produced by accountants so these problems of interpretation should be of concern to them. There is surely something profoundly unsatisfactory about having to make assumptions which are patently false when estimating such presumably economically significant variables as technological progress (e.g Solow, 1957).

Expression (2) appears to be motivated by an intention to describe an empirical law governing the relationship between L, K and O at some level of analysis. If this is the case then some basic questions concerning fundamental measurement principles need to be asked: (i) do the dimensions of the calculation (or more strictly 'derived measurement') make sense? And even more fundamentally, (ii) are the arithmetic relations implied in expressions such as (2) justified as a logical representation of the assumed underlying empirical relations?[9]

---

[8] The defence that accounting measures may be good approximations to their theoretical counterparts is unconvincing in the light of Lancaster and Lipsey (1956-57).

[9] More correctly is it possible to discover a homomorphism between the numerical and empirical relational systems? These principles of good measurement are comprehensively explained in Krantz et al. (1971), Suppes et al. (1989) and Luce et al. (1990).

There is a rule in the theory of physical systems and presumably extends to any system of objectively verifiable measurements that empirically meaningful equations containing variables, which are added or set equal to one another, have to have the same dimensions. This fact helps in the development of valid theory and helps to avoid mistakes. Krantz *et al.* (1971) gives numerous examples of application of the principle applied in the natural sciences.[10] In the practice of scientific management, where financial measures enter equations, exactly the same principles apply assuming, that is, that the notion of cost is accepted as a 'dimension' additional to the familiar physical dimensions of units of product and time.[11] Consequently, if (2) is supposed to embody a maintained empirical law it would be expected that the units in which O is measured would be the same as the units resulting from multiplying together units in which the labour and capital terms are measured (whatever these might be). It is often not clear if the parameters α and β are meant to be 'dimensionless' constants or variables. It might be supposed that their dimensions are such that, in the context of expression (2), they act to convert the RHS units to those on the LHS. However α and β would not then add to give a characterisation of 'degrees of homogeneity' since they are expressed in different units. Such an interpretation of α and β would consequently prevent the usual understanding of these parameters and illustrates some of the problems that arise from considering a rigorous operationalization of (2).

The discipline of thought required by dimensional considerations may be taken a step further by considering the issue of whether (2) embodies a valid representation of an underlying empirical structure. The arithmetic operation of multiplication maps the multiplier and the multiplicand to the product and is equivalent to repeated addition of the multiplicand by a number of times equal to the multiplier. If (2) is to be interpreted in a *fundamental* measurement context, the intuition behind the physical process described in the Cobb-Douglas production function is not clear.[12] Assuming the simplest possible scenario where

---

[10] For instance see the discussion of the partial differential equation describing the propagation of viscosity of a fluid (pp. 457-458 and pp. 479-480).

[11] This point is discussed in a later section of this chapter. The economic order quantity formula is an example of how dimensional analysis works in a social science context. The order quantity has the dimension of units of product, which is the same dimension as that derived from multiplying the cost of one setup by the rate of usage (in units per time) and dividing by carrying charges per unit of time.

[12] Fundamental measurements involve the direct assignment of a number to an object or event based upon carrying through an effective procedure. In physical science an example is the measurement of length by means of rulers. Derived measures, on the other hand, are based upon functions of fundamental measures. These possess significance based upon criteria including whether they reflect an

$A(t)$, α and β are all unity and the operation of addition is interpreted as a 'joining together in a production process', why should a unit of labour (say) be joined together with other identical units of labour K times to produce a unit of output? It could be argued, presumably, that K is an intensity factor. However the unit dimensions which such a position would entail would be inconsistent with the simple additive model of production used to justify the interpretation of the addition operation. Again this shows the importance of establishing what measurements (and thus dimensions) are involved in operationalizing expressions such as (2) and illustrates the not insignificant conceptual difficulties involved in doing so.

Alternatively if expression (2) is treated as a derived measure, the need to find a direct physical interpretation of the multiplication operation is less pressing. However, it still leaves the problem of consistent dimensions unanswered. If the Cobb-Douglas function describes an empirical law (say, reflecting a law of compensation between labour and capital in the production of output) then calculations of the type produced by Solow (1957) might be meaningful. However, the nature of the law constrains the arithmetic operations that can be legally applied to such measures. It is not possible to just add densities together to obtain the densities of two substances, for instance. Ultimately, in practical accounting situations, where random variables are involved, justification for treating the RHS of expression (2) as a derived measurement[13] depends upon its status as a statistic and the extent to which it covaries with the measure of output. It is conceivable, in the absence of a proof to the contrary that (2) might have useful statistical properties, notwithstanding the lack of formal, mathematical aggregative properties. The possibility of interpreting expression (2) as a statistic will be further discussed in a later section.

Interpreting the physical production function on its own evidently raises a number of conceptual issues bearing upon the practice of measurement which appear to have been largely overlooked in the economic theory and econometric literature. However, the physical production function plays its most significant theoretical and practical accounting role in conjunction with cost and profit functions. Under neo-classical assumptions minimization (maximization) of the cost (profit) function subject to the constraints embodied in the physical production function determines the equilibrium levels of output and prices at all levels of aggregation (and thus factor shares). The descriptors 'cost function' and 'profit function' are reserved for

---

empirical law (e.g. density measurement) or have nice statistical properties (e.g. the arithmetic mean). In most disciplines there are only a handful of fundamental measures. Most measures are derived.

[13] 'Derived measurement' is understood here as being defined in the wide sense advocated by Roberts (1979).

relationships involving financial variables and are similar to the constructs measured by accountants. In the context of the variables of K and L already discussed, the cost function to be minimized subject to the technical constraints on production takes the simple and intuitively appealing form:

$$C = rK + wL \qquad (3)$$

Where C is the cost of production in monetary units, and r and w are unit prices of capital and labour respectively. Many of the problems of interpretation which arose with the physical production function are absent from (3) at least at very disaggregated levels. To make this more clear take the general form of (3):

$$C(O) = p_1 I_1 + p_2 I_2 + \ldots + p_n I_n \qquad (4)$$

Where $C(O)$ is the unit cost of output and the p_i are the unit prices of the n inputs that produce one unit of output according to (1). Most importantly, the dimensions of both sides of (4) are clearly the same: costs per unit of output. Applying prices to the individual inputs gives individual total input costs which, when added together, give the total cost of producing one unit of output. The addition operation over costs can be given a rigorous fundamental measurement interpretation (Willett, 1991). Furthermore, measurements of the form of (4) are more easily accessible from accounting records than those of the form of (1), contain all the information contained in the latter, together with additional information about prices and would not, in attempting to estimate output econometrically, automatically lead to the problem of omitted variables. Consequently, in certain respects, despite its apparently greater complexity compared to the form of expressions based on (1), cost functions based on (4) may be a more satisfactory starting point for the analysis of economic behaviour than physical production functions.

This is the strategy adopted in illustrating the possibilities for analysis in the concluding section of this chapter. Before any analysis can begin, however, it is necessary to recount, for the benefit of economists unfamiliar with the accounting literature, a controversy concerning the accounting interpretation of expression (4) which was almost contemporaneous with the capital theory debate and in some ways paralleled its concerns. The issue revolved around whether it makes empirical sense to treat all inputs in the same manner in cost functions if they are long term 'assets' (e.g. the machines used in production which might last for years) or short term assets (e.g. units of an input material consumed in production by using the machine). Ultimately replacing sloppy with precise, statistical reasoning can solve this problem. As will be shown, expression (4) itself, while apparently plausible at first sight is still, as yet, a misleading simplification of an accurate model of reality.

III. PRODUCTION AND COST FUNCTIONS IN ACCOUNTING

It is in the nature of their work that accountants tend to be concerned with cost functions[14] and the measurements with which they are associated rather than physical production functions as such. Nevertheless, given the objective of relating revenues and expenses generated by the firm to its production activities, it would be expected that the accountant would have to implicitly consider the relationship between physical inputs and outputs in production in order to construct performance measures such as accounting earnings (i.e. the 'profit' or 'loss' disclosed in the income statement of firms). Perhaps surprisingly this simple fact has been overlooked in much of the accounting literature in the past two to three decades. An overly close focus on economic theory considerations by accountants trying to understand the theoretical basis of accounting measurement is partly responsible for this omission.

In the accounting literature there are two main competing views on how to best understand what it is that accounting earnings (and asset values) represent to the measurer about the 'real world'.[15] Within the confines of what is referred to as strict 'historic cost accounting' both interpretations amount to much the same thing. However when non-historic cost data is considered, reconciling the two views becomes much more problematic and it becomes more important as to which view is taken as being the proper starting point (i.e. as axiomatic). One view is 'profit and loss account' oriented holding that accounting numbers are the result of 'matching' revenues and expenses in productive activities, produced with the primary purpose of measuring firm or individual performance. The net costs of activities which are finished ('realized') contribute to the profit of the firm in the income statement and costs incurred in activities which are unfinished ('unrealized') are shown in the balance sheet as 'assets' and carried forward to appear in future income statements of the firm. This view is highly descriptive of what accountants actually do when they prepare a set of accounts for a firm and has an old pedigree (e.g. see Littleton, 1953). However it appears to many accounting theorists to lack economic motivation (i.e. what do the resulting accounting numbers tell the user about the economic value

---

[14] It is not intended to distinguish between cost and 'profit' functions. The former will be understood as subsuming the latter, profit functions being interpreted as cost functions with one of the elements reserved for the negative 'cost of revenues' associated with the sale of a unit of output.

[15] In accounting terminology an 'asset' is considered to be something (often a physical object such as land, buildings, machines (sometimes referred to as 'equity')) is reserved by the accountant for the proprietorial interest in the funds which source the assets of the firm (e.g. the share capital and retained reserves of a company limited by shares).

of the firm?). An inability to answer this question has led to a focus upon the alternative 'balance sheet oriented' view of accounting numbers. Under this view the chief objective of accounting information is to establish the proper economic value of assets and the provision of performance measures is a secondary, derivative outcome of that process.

The balance sheet viewpoint draws most of its support in the accounting literature from Hicks' (1946) definition of income. Basically this is interpreted in the firm context as defining income as the difference between the value of a firm's assets at the beginning and end of an accounting period. If values can be clearly and unambiguously associated with assets at different points in time this approach appears to solve the problem of economic motivation referred to above. Unfortunately a little thought shows that this is not the case and that there are additional difficulties with the approach which hinders a clear understanding of what it is that accounting numbers in general represent and, more particularly, what is the nature of accounting cost functions.

One difficulty relates to a lack of objectivity in the basic notion of what is 'value'. The notion of value is typically not well defined under the balance sheet oriented viewpoint in the sense that the object being measured, such as an asset, does not, in general, have a unique value independent of the measurer. Current values attributed to assets, for example, vary according to the valuer and depend upon for whom the asset is supposed to have a value and the time at which the valuation takes place, among other things. Other difficulties relate to the 'measurement' of discounted present values that depends upon speculation about future cash flows, the appropriate discount rate and, crucially, upon the possibility of separating out the future cash flows generated by the asset from those generated by other assets. Attempting to associate changes in assets values with the activities carried on by firms is a tricky issue. It has caused attempts to rationalize the accountant's notions of cost and profit measures to become bogged down in a seemingly fruitless search for meaning in the accountant's practice of provision accounting, the most notable and well known instance of which is the depreciation adjustment.

In the calculation of earnings it is almost always the case that a 'charge for depreciation' is made against income for the period. Economists often have only a vague understanding of what this item represents in practical terms, most usually that it somehow measures the fall in the value of assets over the period of account. This lack of clarity is understandable in view of the fact that accounting standards themselves rationalize the depreciation calculation in this manner, e.g. see IAS4 (IASC, 1974). The most common form of method used to calculate depreciation is the straight line method which essentially takes the difference between the cost of an asset and its expected realizable value and divides this figure by an estimate of the asset's useful life. The amount thus computed is charged against the revenues of successive accounting periods until the cumulated amount charged either exceeds the numerator amount in the above calculation or until the asset is sold, if this is sooner. In the latter case there may be an adjustment to the income statement included in an item sometimes called the 'profit or loss on disposal of assets'. This adjustment (both the depreciation charge and the profit or loss on disposal) is an important element, conceptually if not always practically, in the accounting notion of earnings and thus for the practical estimation of cost functions in economic analysis. Since decisions in practice are made on the basis of the notion of accounting earnings rather than on that of economic earnings, it is important that its nature is properly understood.

The analysis of cost functions in the accounting literature has largely been carried out in the context of functions similar to that shown in expression (4). However 'provision adjustments' such as depreciation are included and assumed to be an attempt to measure one of the elements on the RHS of the function, i.e.:

$$C = p_1 I_1 + p_2 I_2 + \ldots + p_{n-1} I_{n-1} + D \qquad (5)$$

Here the nth element has been replaced by a depreciation charge so that $D = p_n I_n$ is interpreted as being an estimate of, say, the fall in value of a machine due to its being used in production. On this interpretation it becomes necessary to identify both p_n and I_n, the latter being taken to represent some physical measure of the usage of the asset, the former the monetary value of the usage of the asset. Thomas (1969, 1974) showed, by an exhaustive analysis of many different arguments for and against the many different methods of depreciation found in the accounting literature, that it was difficult to attach any sensible meaning to the depreciation adjustment as a measure of the fall in the value of an asset, in part due to the reasons outlined immediately above. Consequently the balance sheet oriented approach to understanding cost and revenue functions in the accounting literature leaves much to be desired in terms of clarifying what is actually being measured. More insight into this issue can be gained by being descriptively accurate about the accounting measurement process, which basically means adopting the alternative transactions based approach to understanding accounting measurement. The form of transaction theory which is described in the following section and used as the basis of the analysis carried out in the remainder of this chapter is called 'Statistical activity cost theory'. Unlike the balance sheet oriented perspective on accounting measurement, it closely models practical accounting measurement techniques and hence it has greater potential to inform economic theorizing about the impact of production and cost functions on economic systems.

IV. COST FUNCTIONS AS MEASURABLE CONCEPTS

Statistical Activity Cost theory formalizes the transactions approach to accounting measurement through a set of axioms. These can be described in a number of different ways and the following is a shortened, intuitive version of the full set of axioms discussed in Willett (1987, 1988) and analyzed rigorously in Willett (1991). The axioms are expressed in deterministic form and the prefix 'Statistical' to 'Activity Cost' refers to the fact that the variables of the theory are interpreted as random variables (*rvs*) in applications. It is these *rvs* (costs, start times and duration times of activities) about which accountants gather statistical information.

There are two basic notions in the theory, a **cost structure** describing the properties of transaction costs, and a **production structure**, describing the properties of production relations. These two structures provide the fundamental data measured by accountants. A cost is defined as the debt created by the transfer of a resource set between two accounting entities in an interval of time. The value attached to the cost is the observed debt agreed between the parties to the transaction and is additive under certain, clearly specified, general conditions. A production relation is an ascertained binary relation between one resource set at one point in time (the input) and another at a 'just noticeable' later point in time (the output). A string of production relations forms a matching relation between a number of resource sets creating an equivalence class of 'matched' resource sets, the aggregated cost of which defines the concept of an 'activity cost'.

The most non-obvious axioms and constructs describing the properties of costs and production relations may be summarized as follows. **An accounting space** is a system of *rvs* that takes for granted the properties of physical and time measurement, the obvious properties of debt relationships and the physical aspects of production processes. In particular, the following three axioms are satisfied. (1) **The additivity of costs:** The debt value characterizing numerical costs is additive when exactly one of the components of cost (i.e., the two accounting entities between which the debt exists, the resource set and the time interval) is entirely distinct and the others are identical or the entity components are reversed. This axiom establishes the conditions under which costs can be added together and it justifies not only additivity of financial statements over time but also the 'consolidation' of financial statements referred to in the concluding section of this chapter. (2) **The continuity of production relations:** If an accounting entity holds a resource at two points in time without a change of ownership then that entity owns that resource continually over the time interval. This enables the matching of revenues against expenses to take place over an extended period of time. (3) **The separability of production relations:** If a smaller production relation is contained within a larger production relation then the resources remaining also form a production relation. This axiom allows the separate costing of activities of short and long term duration. As indicated above, costs are 'matched' in activities if there is some sequence of production relations linking them together. The matching relation is an equivalence relation and partitions the resource sets of firms and economies into mutually exclusive 'activities'. Activity costs are aggregates of the individual transaction costs (valued by debt) accruing in activities.

The construction of activity costs using these elemental notions therefore leads to the identification of firms as being collections of (non-overlapping) activity costs (which account for all of the firm's costs) and of the characterization of economies as being collections of measurable accounting entities. The 'physical' aspect of an activity cost, i.e. the 'activity' itself, is, in some ways, analogous to the physical production function of economic theory but does not necessarily lend itself to characterization in terms of a mathematical function. The traditional notion of a production function both as it appears to be perceived in economic theory (and in the balance sheet oriented valuation approach to understanding this concept) is as a one-to-one or many-to-one function. For example, in a process producing two sheets of metal, 10 minutes of labour and 1 kilogram of metal slab might produce 2 sheets using a rolling machine. This would typically be envisaged as a many-to-one relation, three inputs giving one output. In trying to construct objective, reliable measures of costs and profits for decision making in the real world, the difficulty this interpretation creates is the 'allocation' problem referred to above, i.e., the need to attribute a part of the cost or fall in value of the fixed asset (the rolling machine in this case) to each item of output produced.

In the approach taken using Statistical Activity Cost theory, the nature of the measurement process is interpreted differently. The production relation in the example just cited is interpreted as being a many-to-many function with two physical outputs, including a fixed output, the rolling machine, as well as the variable output, the two metal slabs. This is a more accurate description of the physical relationship between the inputs and outputs in the process described and better corresponds with reality whenever fixed assets emerge changed physically only to a negligible extent from the effect of producing one more unit of output. A many-to-many production relation of this type is then further interpreted as being separable into two production relations, one relating the 10 minutes of labour and the 1 kilogram metal slab to the two sheets of metal, the other relating the rolling machine to itself over time. The latter production relation may be characterized as being part of the activity of holding or using the fixed asset. This rule provides a conceptual basis for the separate 'costing' of fixed assets, which can then be averaged over time and thus aggregated with other costs having the same time dimension. This point will be returned to below.

As an example of how activities are constructed, suppose that each sheet of metal produced in the previously described production relation is used with 5 minutes of additional labour time to produce a metal disc. Denoting the inputs as A_1 (5 minutes of labour), A_2 (1/2 kilogram metal slab), A_3 (1 metal sheet), A_4 (5 minutes labour) and A_5 (1 metal disc) and using the recursive rule that a resource belongs to an activity if and only if it is either the input or the output of another resource in the activity, the activity based upon the output A_5 with respect to the relevant time interval is defined as being the equivalence class $\{A_1, ..., A_5\}$. The activity cost of activity A_5 is simply the sum of the transaction costs of the individual resource sets and accounting numbers are functions of sums of activity costs. It is therefore easy to see, since inputs and costs are both outcomes of essentially random processes (technical and market) why accounting numbers which activity costs are used to construct may be most generally described as 'functions of random sums of random numbers'.[16]

These illustrations show the application of Statistical Activity Cost theory to production and cost functions at the most microscopic level of analysis. It is a level of analysis that is usually not of a great deal of interest or concern to an economist. However, if this theory of accounting measurement is indeed an accurate numerical representation of real world attributes, these 'atomic level' elements must eventually aggregate to provide the basis for the kind of production functions which enter in micro-economic and ultimately macro-economic analysis. The idea of a *measurable economy* consisting of a collection of dated activity costs may be understood in the following manner.

All the resources of an economy are partitioned into activities by the matching relation. Firms are simply subsets of collections of these activities and financial statements are systematic records based upon all the transactions costs of particular firms classified into activities up to some point in time. This representation is useful as a basic framework for understanding accounting measurements and the relation of the accountant's concept of production and cost functions to the economist's concepts because it allows one to see how the fundamental measures of accounting are used to construct derived accounting measures. Activities start, continue and finish over a period of time and the value of accounting performance measures (the most important of which is accounting 'earnings' shown in the income statement) are ultimately determined by recognition rules based upon primary

---

[16] This description of the way in which accounting measurements are carried out and accounting numbers are constructed may seem obvious. Certainly it is not a very complicated process. However the mechanics just described, which can be used to inform us of the statistical properties of accounting numbers, are totally ignored in the alternative balance sheet viewpoint of accounting measurement referred to earlier.

measurements of these variables.[17] This is a particularly important point for the economist to appreciate. The accountant's earnings function is one of the best known examples of a derived accounting measure and it comes as close as any accounting number to what the economist would consider to be a cost or profit function.

In calculating accounting earnings in practice, activities are conventionally divided into two distinct categories, short term (which can be operationalised as having an expected duration time of less than one accounting period) and long term (which have expected duration times greater than one accounting period). Instances of short term activities are things such as the regular purchase, processing and resale of a commodity or an overhead expense such as a rental payment, whereas a long term activity is illustrated by the purchase, holding and disposal of a machine used for manufacturing the commodity. The six main time states that an activity can take with respect to an accounting period beginning at $t-1$ and finishing at t are: (a) Start and finish before $t-1$; (b) Start before $t-1$ and finish after $t-1$ but before t (i.e. during the accounting period); (c) Start before $t-1$ and finish after t: (d) Start during and finish during the accounting period; (e) Start during the accounting period and finish after t; (f) Start and finish after t. The way the net costs (revenues less expenses) of an activity enter into the accounting earnings function (are recognized) depends upon whether the activity is short or long term and its time state. The calculation rule is described, with some simplifications, in expression (6), which shows, in a relatively mechanistic way, the rules for determining the value of the earnings function H at time t, $H|t$, over k different types of activity class:

$$H|t = H'|t + H''|t$$

where

$$H' = \begin{cases} \sum_k \sum_j^{N''} C_j \text{ if } S_j < T_i, T_i - 1 < S_j + D_j \leq T_i \text{ and } D_R \leq 1. \\ 0 \text{ otherwise} \end{cases}$$

---

[17] Conventional accounting measurement associates start times with the date of the first purchase invoice and finish time with the date of the last sales invoice. Other possibilities, such as cash settlement dates, exist however.

$$H''|t = \begin{cases} \sum_k \sum_j^{N''_1} c_k / d_k \text{ if } S_j < T_i < S_j + D_j, T_i - S_j < D_k \text{ and } D_k > 1 \\ \sum_k \sum^{N''_2} C_j - \min\{(T_i - 1 - S_j), d_k\} \times c_k / d_k \text{ if } T - 1 < S_j + D_j < T_i \\ \text{and} \\ 0 \text{ otherwise, if } D_k > 1 \end{cases}$$

(6)

This formula assumes straight line depreciation is calculated. $H'|t$ is the contribution for the accounting period. $H''|t$ is the provision accounting calculation. N' is the number of short term activities finishing in the period. N''_1 is the number of unfinished long term activities at T_i and N''_2 is the number of long term activities finishing in the period. C_j and C_k are the random costs in the respective activities and the S and D variables represent the random start duration times of the activities. The lower case c and d stand for the expected costs and duration times of the activities.

Expression (6) emphasizes two points about accounting calculations. Firstly they are essentially random functions. The description of production relations and costs stated earlier may have given the impression that accountants know these with certainty. In some, rare, simple cases they do but in general they do not. While the cost of a set of items purchased through a single invoice, for example, is often known, the individual elements in the invoice may enter into different activities and their individual costs may not be known. Furthermore the problem of joint processes in some circumstances makes it possible to estimate a per unit cost only by analogy with some equivalent 'separable' process for producing the same product. The latter may or may not exist. Consequently there is an inherent uncertainty in most accounting measurements which is in addition to the natural chance variations occurring in the costs of inputs and outputs and in the physical measures of inputs and outputs themselves. Such considerations necessitate a probabilistic interpretation of accounting calculations.

Secondly, related to the first point and mentioned earlier, the formulation of accounting numbers illustrated in expression (6) and implied by Figure 5 is that any accounting number, including accurate cost functions will be some function (or an estimate of some function) of a random sum of random numbers. The key variables contained in the random sums are activity costs and the start times and duration times of the activities. More formally any accounting number, $A(t)$, may be described as:

$$A(t) = f(C(t), S(t), D(t), X_i), i = 1 \text{ to } n \tag{7}$$

$C(t)$ representing the costs incurred in activities, $S(t)$ the start times of the activities and $D(t)$ the duration times. The X_i variables represent a list of decision variables that are used to 'manipulate' the measure, possibly to provide it with enhanced statistical properties (e.g. estimates of the length of life of fixed assets).

The actual form of cost functions to which this theory leads to is somewhat different from those described in both (4) and (5). The random variable characterization requires the assumption of a multiplicative form for the relationship between p_n and I_n to be replaced by the discrete convolution of prices or costs over the random number of relevant inputs and outputs, i.e.,

$$Y(t) = \sum_k \sum_{j=1}^{j=Ij(i)} \sum_{i=1}^{i=Ni(t)} p_{ijk} + D_{jk}(t) \tag{8}$$

Here $Y(t)$ is the earnings of a firm in period t, k is the number of distinct activities pursued by the firm in that period,[18] $I_j(t)$ is the number of activities of class j completed in period t, p_{ijk} is the price (cost) of the ith input of the jth output of the kth activity. $D_{jk}(t)$ is the depreciation charge for the jth realization or output of the kth activity. If the activity is of the short term duration type $D_{jk}(t)$ is always zero but otherwise varies according to the functional form of D. More will be said about the depreciation function in the following section. Mostly in practice it takes one or two specific forms based upon the elapsed time of the activity.

For the economist interested in working with empirical measurements of actual cost data from reported financial statements there are a number of points to note. First, in an income statement $Y(t)$ would be the income figure before distributions (which are discretionary) and ideally there would be a maximum of k accounts in the income statement summing to $Y(t)$. In actuality many of the different k activities would be lumped together into more aggregated 'accounts'. Even worse poor measurement practices and arbitrary, *ad hoc* judgements would further tend to obscure the cause and effect relationships underlying the activity cost concept. Nevertheless on average and particularly with large samples, financial statement information interpreted in this manner should provide reasonable starting point estimates of firm cost functions of the type shown in expression (8).

---

[18] As before, some activities create a product for resale, some are short term overhead activities and some are longer term activities such as the purchase and holding of machines.

Second, in formulating this theory about what accounting numbers represent, nothing whatsoever has been assumed about market structures (e.g. whether markets are perfectly competitive) or about the supposed rationality of decision-makers. The only assumptions made are as stated in the axioms and implied by the intended interpretation of the concepts. The fact that the variables of the model are assumed to be random is important. The probabilistic interpretation of economic measurement which it supposes, focuses attention on accounting numbers as statistics which can be used to estimate interesting parameters of the economic process which generates numbers such as $Y(t)$. Thus, for example, accurately estimating the correct form of $Y(t)$ from empirical data (including the probability forms of the stochastic processes in (8)) becomes important for both understanding and predicting the profitability of firms and for more general questions such as how prices and quantities of products might be determined.

Third, in general, the variables $I_j(t)$ and p_{ij} are not independent *rvs*. With perfectly competitive markets these *rvs* would be independent and certain simplifications follow from this fact. However in the simplest case, even when these variables are independent, expression (8) as a random function leads to different distributional and moment related consequences compared to those which would follow from expression (4) if the relevant variables in that expression were to be interpreted as *rvs*. Some of these differences will be discussed in the following section and they demonstrate that the distinction between the forms of (4), (5) and (8) are far from trivial both in theoretical and empirical contexts.

Finally, it is not usually sensible to assume, except in very restricted circumstances, that in any decision analysis meant to inform policy, the physical variables $I_j(t)$ and $N_i(t)$ can be meaningfully separated from the financial variables p_{ij}. Functional forms of the type described by (1) may be technologically sound at a point in time but in a dynamic context over time as long as one accounting period the form would change depending upon variations in costs (for example, through competitive behaviour). Consequently it is unrealistic in empirical contexts to expect to be able to extract the marginal forms of the physical and financial random variables in (8) so as to form useful and meaningful, separate production functions.

The implications of this accounting approach to measuring and understanding production and cost functions are statistical rather than economic, in the sense that the theory says little if anything that is profound about economic behaviour. Expression (8) is a very general theory of cost functions in the real world. The behavioural implications which follow from using such a theory in analyzing economic systems, however, comes from the specific hypotheses which may be imposed on the distributional forms of the cost, start time and duration time variables and the dynamic relationships which are theorized to hold between these values over time. The next section considers some of the statistical implications of this theory for economic analysis.

V. STATISTICAL IMPLICATIONS OF THE DESCRIPTIVE ACCOUNTING INTERPRETATION OF PRODUCTION AND COST FUNCTIONS

i) Production functions

Despite the proviso about the inseparability of physical and financial variables in the cost function and of the known problems with the use of the physical production functions in economic analysis the possibility remains open that certain functional forms (such as the Cobb Douglas discussed earlier) might possess nice statistical properties which provide them with useful estimation properties. As noted earlier studies that have used the Cobb Douglas production function at highly aggregated data levels have been criticized in the economic literature and it is worthwhile now considering this criticism from an accounting-statistical viewpoint.

From the microscopic level of analysis at which accounting measurement takes place, production functions of the Cobb Douglas type do not make sense as directly observable production sequences or any activities in the way they are defined in Statistical Activity Cost theory. Economists' production functions are more like technological laws expressing production possibilities among different activities. If physical activities of the accounting type were to be described as mathematical functions, intuition would suggest representing the relevant production sequence as an additive sum. For example the activity described in the example given earlier might be represented as:

$$O = 0.5I_1 + 5I_2 + 2I_3 \tag{9}$$

Where the symbols and units are interpreted in the obvious manner.[19]

Whether or not this representation can be justified (in terms of its supposed dimensions and arithmetic properties) however, it clearly bears no resemblance mathematically to the form of the Cobb Douglas function shown in (2). The accounting measurement of an activity takes place at a point in time and requires fixed input coefficients and constant returns to scale.[20] Possibly the best way to understand the economists' production function in terms of accounting measurements,

---

[19] There is nothing obvious about the units analysis, however. Presumably the coefficient is not dimensionless. One way of solving the problem of dimensions referred to in section 2 would be for the units on the coefficient of I_i to be of the form $O/I_i|E_ja_jI_j$, i=j, i.e. 'Output per unit of input I_i given the other inputs and their coefficients in the production process'. However logically there are probably a number of equally plausible alternative solutions to this problem.

[20] This is not strictly speaking a logically consistent statement since any change at all requires some time for the change to take place.

therefore, is a function describing isoquants passing through the most efficient activities in an industry. This is essentially the same as the Linear Programming interpretation of the production function which is well known to economists (e.g. see Blaug, 1997, pp 412-7) and fits nicely into an accounting framework. The rays from the origin in the LP version of the economists' isoquant may be understood as representing the accountants' notion of activities and points on the discrete form of the isoquant represent the points of maximum efficiency for the level of output described by the isoquant. Other points on activities above the isoquant, away from the origin, denote less efficient processes and would be typically scattered in a cloud in KL space. Thanks to a variety of causes including random events, such activities might survive, for example, by fortuitously being more profitable than 'efficient' activities due to changes in the relative prices of labour and capital. The isoquant of the economists' production function therefore may be interpreted as being the lower bound of a scatter plot of points on measurable accounting activities in KL space. Testing any particular form of empirical production function would presumably need to use information about the spatial pattern of the sample points contained in the relevant scatter plot.

The Cobb Douglas production function has two very useful characteristics as a potential descriptor of such an efficient technological boundary. First it allows activities with fixed input coefficients and constant returns to scale to be basic building blocks of the processes it purports to describe. Second it provides, through appropriate choice of parameters, a wide range of trade-offs between different activities in describing the mix of activities. As such the Cobb Douglas production function gives a convenient basis for testing the plausible economic hypothesis that the technologies in a competitive industry are chosen in such a way that there is an inverse relationship between labour hours and machine hours in equivalent production activities at the efficient frontier. This is presumably the intuition behind the application of 'production functions' in much empirical research.

It is evident from this discussion of some of the problems of operationalizing economic theory through accounting measurements that care is needed in distinguishing between the concept of an activity or production sequence at a point in time and the economists notion of a 'production function', which purports to describe an economic 'law' based upon complex behavioural considerations. In the sense used here, accounting activities are nothing more and nothing less than the simple concepts described above and illustrated in the preceding examples. It is unclear that the measurable construct with which accountants are concerned requires a mathematical representation like (9) and it may even be misleading. The production function of economic theory, however, describes a maintained economic 'law' and the needs of analysis demand a mathematical representation.

From a purely theoretical point of view, the notion of a production function of the Cobb Douglas kind, *at the level of analysis of the industry*, fits neatly into a Statistical Activity Cost theory characterization of accounting 'activities'. Relationships of the kind postulated by the Cobb Douglas production function are potentially testable through the observation of accounting activities. It is less clear that the presumption that mathematical forms of production functions such as Cobb Douglas can be assumed at more aggregated levels and specifically at the macro-economic level of analysis. This has been done in empirical contexts and criticized mainly from a mathematical viewpoint in the economics literature. As stated earlier, the issue in this context really seems to be a statistical and inferential one that resolves into two questions. On the one hand if Cobb Douglas functional forms or something similar are good models of the technological relationships between inputs and outputs at the micro-level of analysis, does that allow the inference that a similar relationship holds at highly aggregated levels? On the other hand, does the identification of a Cobb Douglas form of production function at an aggregated level of analysis allow the inference that micro production functions are of this type?

In general, from computer simulation experiments, the answer appears to be negative. By generating large numbers of simulated random variables, O, based upon the functional form in (1) with random values for both K and L, it is possible to fit Cobb Douglas production functions to the aggregated values of K, L and O in some instances. However even in those instances where it is possible to do this and the aggregated model appears to have a Cobb Douglas form it is usually significantly biased in its estimate of total output and the estimated aggregate parameters usually do not reflect the conditions of the micro-functions.[21] This point is presumably similar to that made by Fisher (1969). Conversely it is well known that aggregate Cobb Douglas forms can be generated by non-Cobb Douglas forms (e.g. see Heathfield and Wibe, pp 90-1).

On the basis of this analysis, the Cobb Douglas production function appears to have theoretical plausibility as a potentially scientific description of production relationships at the middle level of economic analysis. There is also some occasional empirical support for modeling Cobb Douglas production functions at the micro-level of analysis. Consequently, given the apparently good fit which is often achieved empirically in the study of aggregated production functions of this type even with cross-sectional data (e.g. Mizon, 1977) it seems that, from an accounting-statistical perspective, it is the statistical theory of the

---

[21] For example in simulations carried out by the author the aggregation of 'constant returns' micro-functions typically returned 'increasing returns' aggregated models of Cobb Douglas. A multiplicative error term form of Cobb Douglas was assumed in the estimation of the aggregated function.

aggregation of production functions which needs to be addressed in research, rather than any discomfiture with the notion of a physical production function as such, aggregated or otherwise.

ii) Cost functions

It is not often appreciated in economic theory how important and crucial is the time element in measuring activity costs. All products take some time to make but the time period is, in general, different for each product. In principal it should be possible to discover a form of expression (2) for the cost or profit of any product. However because time is potentially money it is not possible to compare products for their relative profitability unless it is known over what periods of time it takes to produce the products. Product A realizing a profit of $10 in one day is better, other things equal, than product B realizing a profit of $10 in two days. Consequently an operationalization of the concept of profit or income has to encompass the dimension of time as well as cost for it to be useful in decision and policy contexts. This explains the difference in form between expressions (4) and (8). The accountant is required to compute an earnings figure for an accounting period despite the fact that many activities straddle the beginning and end of the period. Consequently it is necessary to estimate the activity cost per accounting period (i.e. per unit of time) which explains the appearance of the depreciation calculation in (8) in the place of a convolution term for a consumed input.

Economists are aware that cost functions have to be estimated on the basis of sample data in most instances. The convolution terms in (8) are random variables and sample data could be used to estimate their average values along with other parameters of the underlying processes. However the essentially statistical nature of accounting earnings as an estimator of the long term average cost function of the firm and the part played by the depreciation calculation and other accounting allocations does not appear to be well understood at the theoretical level by either accountants or economists. The characteristics of the profitability and cost per unit of time of an activity, a collection of activities or a firm can only be known with certainty and measured directly when the activity is completed or the firm liquidated. One way of interpreting the accounting earnings function, therefore is as a time dependent estimate of this ultimate, direct measure. A two period, one product firm, for example, might buy a machine for $6 and expend a further $4 on input costs in period 1, selling one unit of output for $10 in period 1 and one for $12 in period 2, scrapping the machine at the end of the second period. The lifetime profit of the firm is $(22-4-6) = $12. This was earned over two periods so that the time rate of profitability is $6. This rate is unknown at the end of the first accounting period and standard statistical criteria thus suggests that the best earnings estimate for that period is one which, on average, is closest to $6. As the convolution terms are fixed in the form of (8) the D term is important because it can be manipulated to give the best estimate of the chosen parameter with respect to some statistical criteria. With hindsight and adopting the accounting accrual convention of only recognizing the profit from an activity when it is complete (i.e. sold) D in period 1 should therefore be chosen to be $(10-2-3) = \$5$, assuming straight line depreciation is used. In period 2 the accrual earnings would then also be $(12-2-3) = \$7$, the last term in parentheses being the remaining depreciation of the cost of the machine to be written off. If depreciation had not been charged and the cost of the machine had been 'written off' in the first period, the earnings estimate of profitability would have been $(10-2-6) = \$2$ in period 1 and $(12-2) = \$10$ in period 2, obviously inferior as a mean square error estimator of long term profitability, in this instance.

Clearly in the real world, where accountants do not have the benefit of hindsight, this illustration of the pragmatic devices which accountants use in measuring costs overstates the benefits of adjustments such as depreciation. Indeed poor practices in calculating accounting allocations can make matters worse, not better. However it can be shown that, in some circumstances at least, it is possible to compute *ex ante* the best functional form for D according to specific statistical criteria. This calls for more intricate mathematical models and analysis. Consider, for example, the following expression which details how D is calculated over time for a particular class of activities:

$$D(t) = \sum_{i=0}^{\infty} [\alpha(i) - \alpha(i-1)] M(i,t) - \sum_{j=1}^{\infty} \alpha(j-1) Q(j,t) \quad (10)$$

$\alpha(i)$ is the accumulated charge for depreciation per activity by time i, $M(i,t)$ is the number of activities unfinished at t beginning i periods prior to t and $Q(j,t)$ is the number of activities finishing in the period $t-1$ to t.[22]

This is a more succinct way of describing the earnings function in expression (6) and permits derivation of the optimal forms for D. Lane and Willett (1997) show that if start time for activities are governed by a Poisson process and duration times by an exponential law then the optimal form of D in the minimum mean square error sense as an estimator of the long term profitability of the process generating costs is that α should have the form:

---

[22] The first sum in (10) is the current period's depreciation for continuing activities. The second sum is the total cost of completed activities plus the previous accumulated depreciation written back on activities completed in the accounting period.

$$\alpha(i) = \mu_c(1 - d^{i+1})$$
$$\text{where } d = \left(1 - \sqrt{1-p}\right)/p \text{ and } p = e^{-\theta} \tag{11}$$

Although the form of D given in this instance is a global optimum and would not be familiar to practicing accountants it is apparent from simulation experiments that the methods of depreciation used in practice give results that are quite probably insignificantly different from the global optimum. Analysis suggests that if the estimated residual values and useful lives of assets are accurate the accountant's earnings function described in expression (8) should give a reasonable approximation to the long-term profit function of the firm. Economists and econometricians should beware, however, of the political pressures on accountants. These, together with a lack of awareness of the statistical properties of the numbers accountants construct, often lead calculations of D (and of many other instances of cost allocations) to be based not upon best estimating considerations but upon *ad hoc* attempts to manipulate the annual profit figure. In carrying out empirical work on cost functions using published or other accounting information, therefore, as much as is possible should be ascertained about the allocations made in computing the accounting earnings figure. Accounting earnings has the potential to serve the economist but sloppy and amateurish practices in the preparation of financial statements could easily undermine its value.

Data obtained from published financial statements is usually 'consolidated', i.e. data is aggregated across companies that are controlled by a 'holding' company and form a 'group'. Often, especially with large multinational companies, the results and assets of 'associates' and 'joint ventures' are included in the group accounts along with those of 'subsidiary' companies. There are a number of different methods of reporting aggregated data and some of these affect the bottom line figure of earnings. Subject to the simplifications referred to earlier, expression (8) is an accurate descriptor of consolidated earnings before the subtraction of the item 'minority interests share of profits for the year' and before taking into account the 'share of the results of associated companies and joint ventures'. The main problem for the researcher is obtaining detailed line item data, which may not be available in published reports. If the results of associates and joint ventures are included in group accounts, typically only a proportionate share of the associate's or joint venturer's earnings will be included in the consolidated accounts. Consequently if such data is used to estimate cost functions it is probably best to eliminate or make adjustments for both of the latter amounts. Realistically, empirical research on cost functions using accounting data is best done through access to management accounting information where the type of detail required to estimate the key variables in (8) is most likely to be available.

'To consolidate' means to take the financial statements of individual firms in a group and add them together line by line after making adjustments for inter-company transactions. Obeying the rule of addition described in axiom 1 of Table 1 achieves this result. The consolidated profit and loss account is constructed in this way and achieves the result of producing an income statement which is exactly the same as one which would be produced by applying accounting measurement procedures to the group as a whole from scratch. Consequently the problems with the aggregation of functional form which were present in the discussion of the economist's physical production function are absent from analysis based upon cost functions. The principle reason for this is that the former are based upon behavioural considerations arising from complex social interaction (i.e. the hypothesis of a trade off between man hours and machine hours in available technologies) and are not simply measurements of static technologies as such. Accounting cost functions do not involve similar behavioural considerations. They are measures of the outcomes of technological and social processes but they do not depend upon assumptions similar to the trade off hypothesis referred to above. It is only when cost functions are used in conjunction with behavioural hypotheses such as profit maximization to produce functional forms for models predicting or explaining a particular state of affairs that aggregation of the behavioural functions becomes a problem. Thus, for example, in a two firm group, in which the firms bought and sold each other's products, their cost functions could be consolidated to produce the cost function of the group. However aggregating the separate calculations of an expression for the optimum output of each firm would not necessarily produce the optimum output for the group as a whole, especially if decision making were decentralized. The 'aggregation problem' in economic theory is therefore nothing to do with measurement as such but is caused by the complexities involved in attempting to reconcile behavioural models of micro with macro-economic systems.

REFERENCES

Bairam, E.I. (1994), *Homogeneous nonhomogeneous production functions*, Avebury.

Blaug, M. (1997), *Economic theory in retrospect*, 5th edn, Cambridge University Press.

Fisher, F.M. (1969), The existence of aggregate production functions, *Econometrica*, Vol 37, pp 553-577.

Gibbins, M. and Willett, R.J. (1991), The measurement theoretic and statistical properties of the transactions theory of accounting numbers, *Proceedings of the Accounting Association of Australia and New Zealand*, Brisbane, July, pp. 12-21.

Gibbins, M. and Willett, R.J. (1997), New light on accrual, aggregation and allocation, using an axiomatic analysis of accounting numbers, fundamental statistical character, *Abacus*, Vol. 33, No. 2, pp 137-167.

Heathfield, D.F. and Wibe, S. (1987), *An introduction to cost and production functions*, Humanities Press International Inc.

Hicks, J.R. (1946), *Value and capital*, 2nd edn, Clarendon Press.

IASC (1974,) Depreciation, International Accounting Standards Committee.

Krantz, D.H., Luce, R.D., Suppes, P. and Tversky, A. (1971), *Foundations of measurement: additive and polynominal representations*, Vol. 1, Academic Press.

Lancaster, K. and Lipsey, R.G. (1956-57), The general theory of the second best, *Review of Economic Studies*, Vol. 24, pp 11-32.

Lane, J. and Willett, R.J. (1997), Depreciation need not be arbitrary, *Accounting and Business Research*, Vol. 27, pp 179-194.

Luce, R.D., Krantz, D.H., Suppes, P. and Tversky, A. (1990), *Foundations of measurement: representation, axiomatization and invariance*, Vol 3, Academic Press.

Littleton, A.C. (1953), *Structure of accounting theory*, American Accounting Association.

Mizon, G.E. (1977), Inferential procedures in non linear models: An application in a UK industrial cross section study of factor substitution and returns to scale, *Econometrica*, Vol. 45, pp 1221-1241.

Roberts, F.S. (1979), Measurement theory in the *Encyclopedia of Mathematics and its Applications*, Vol 7, ed. Gian-Carlo Rota, Addison-Wesley.

Robinson (1956), *The accumulation of capital*, Macmillan.

Samuelson, P.A. (1962), Parable and realism in capital theory: the surrogate production function, *Review of Economic Studies*, Vol. 39, pp 193-206.

Solow, R.M. (1957), Technical progress and productivity change, *Review of Economics and Statistics*, Vol 39, pp 312-320.

Sraffa, P. (1960), *Production of commodities by means of commodities, prelude to a critique of economic theory*, Cambridge University Press.

Suppes, P., Krantz, D.M., Luce, R. and Tversky, A. (1989), *Foundations of measurement: geometrical, threshold and probabilistic representations*, Vol 2, Academic Press.

Thomas, A. (1969), The allocation problem, *Studies in Accounting Research No. 3*, American Accounting Association.

Thomas, A. (1974), The allocation problem – part two, *Studies in Accounting Research No. 9*, American Accounting Association.

Willett, R.J. (1987), An axiomatic theory of accounting measurement, *Accounting and Business Research*, Vol. 17, Spring, pp 155-171.

Willett, R.J. (1988), An axiomatic theory of accounting measurement – Part Two, *Accounting and Business Research*, Winter.

Willett, R.J. (1991), An axiomatic theory of accounting measurement structures, *IMA Journal of Mathematics Applied in Business Industry*, Vol. 3, pp 45-59.

3 Production versus Cost Functions: Unreliability of the Duality Theorem in Accounting and Economics

Erkin I. Bairam and
Emel Kahya

I. INTRODUCTION

Ever since Shephard's introduction of the 'duality theorem' there have been many attempts to estimate production functions indirectly via cost minimising conditions in accounting and economics (see, *inter alia*, Uzawa (1964), Shephard (1970) and Bairam (1994)). The main point of taking such indirect routes to the production parameter estimation is that one utilizes other types of data (i.e. prices and costs) instead of, or in addition to, data on inputs and output. Unfortunately, it is rarely emphasised that one can relate the cost function's estimates to the parameters of the production function estimates if and only if one is willing to rely on often unrealistic assumptions concerning behaviour – such as cost minimisation under perfect competition.

The main difficulty with such approaches adopted on the basis of theoretical framework by Shephard (1970) is that they always ignore practical problems. For example, if one examines the cross-section jail data which were used by Hayes and Millar (1990) and Mensah and Li (1993) and will be used here, to estimate the production function parameter estimates, some of the problems that accountants and economists prefer to forget become very clear. In this data set (see Mensah and Li (1993), p. 86) price variations were probably obtained because of regional differences. So Hayes and Millar (1990) and Mensah and Li (1993) assumed smooth *ex post* substitution possibilities which led to production function parameter estimates via translog cost functions. However, on the basis of their implicit assumptions, this is very dubious. The main problem follows from the rational assumption that producers (in this case prison authorities) take into account future, as well as current, input and output prices when deciding which production function to choose from among the possibilities implied by the *ex ante* function. Thus, in general one cannot expect to find cost minimising (or profit maximising) conditions holding between inputs, output and *observed* prices. For instance, it is well known that by using a condition where the marginal rate of substitution is related to current relative prices between capital and labour (see, for example, Hayes and Millar (1990)), one gets a biased inference about *ex ante* production function. If investors/producers expect the wage rate to increase, the researcher will underrate the marginal productivity of labour in the *ex ante* function (see Bairam (1994)).

Adding to this inadequacy of *current* prices and costs in estimating production function parameters, duality (Shephard (1970)) between cost and production functions may not hold because cost minimisation may not be the main motive. For instance, looking at the jail data under consideration here, the earlier authors (Hayes and Millar (1990) and Mensah and Li (1993)) freely admit that the 'jail industry' is non-competitive. But if this is accepted, then cost minimisation may not be the main objective of prison authorities.[23] Consequently, cost functions may not yield appropriate (technological) production function parameters.

In this paper, the authors will attempt to double check some of the *cost function* results obtained by Hayes and Millar (1990) and Mensah and Li (1993) by estimating flexible *production functions*. In particular, they will compare/examine the economies of scale estimates obtained from cost functions employed by previous authors and production functions reported in this study and try to assess the reliability of the duality assumption when it is used for non-competitive industries in accounting and economics.

II. THE MODEL AND ESTIMATION PROCEDURES

In the production literature, without an *a priori* test, it is often assumed production functions are homogeneous. Unfortunately, it is not generally known that the homogeneity (and, hence, constant scale elasticity, (CES)) assumption is not an appropriate assumption for most aspects of the production theory (see Bairam (1994)). The new CES function which will be used here, unlike the conventional CES function (Arrow *et al.* (1961)) used in the literature, is *not* homogeneous. This function has been introduced by Bairam (1991a and b) and is specified as a general Box-Cox (1964) two input model:

$$f(Q_i) = \alpha_0 + \beta_1 f(L_i) + \beta_2 f(K_i) \tag{1}$$

---

[23] For example, in the context of prisons, security of prisoners and prison guards may be the main objective, regardless of the costs.

$$f(X_i) = \left[\left(X_i^\lambda - 1\right)/\lambda\right] \text{ and } \alpha_0, \beta_1, \beta_2 \geq 0$$

where Q_i, L_i, K_i are levels of output, labour and capital, respectively.

This function includes as a special case the Cobb-Douglas and Leontief production functions. When $\lambda = 0$, it is reduced to the log-linear function:[24]

$$\ln Q_i = A + \beta_1 \ln L_i + \beta_2 \ln K_i \qquad (2)$$

where $A = \ln \alpha_0$. When $\lambda = 1$, it collapses to the linear function:

$$Q_i = A + \beta_1 L_i + \beta_2 K_i \qquad (3)$$

where $A = (1 + \alpha_0 - \beta_1 - \beta_1)$

This production function has the following marginal productivity properties:

$$(\partial Q_i / \partial L_i) = \beta_1 (L_i / Q_i)^{\lambda-1} \geq 0 \qquad (4)$$

$$(\partial Q_i / \partial K_i) = \beta_2 (K_i / Q_i)^{\lambda-1} \geq 0 \qquad (5)$$

and

$$(\partial^2 Q_i / \partial L_i^2) = \beta_1 (L_i / Q_i)^{\lambda-1} L_i^{-1}(1-\lambda)\left[\beta_1(L_i / Q_i)^{\lambda-1}\right] \gtreqless 0 \qquad (6)$$

$$(\partial^2 Q_i / \partial K_i^2) = \beta_1 (K_i / Q_i)^{\lambda-1} K_i^{-1}(1-\lambda)\left[\beta_2(K_i / Q_i)^{\lambda-1}\right] \gtreqless 0 \qquad (7)$$

Therefore, it is clear from equations (4) and (5) that the marginal products of labour and capital are non-negative. Furthermore, as long as $\lambda < 1$, $\beta_1 (L_i / Q_i)^\lambda$, $\beta_2 (K_i / Q_i)^\lambda > 1$, equation (1) satisfies second order requirements of a neo-classical production function namely $(\partial^2 Q_i / \partial L_i^2)$, $(\partial^2 Q_i / \partial K_i^2) < 0$ (see Chapter 1).

---

[24] This is because, using the Taylor series of expansion, it can be shown that when $\lambda \to 0$, $[X_i^\lambda - 1]/\lambda \to \ln X_i$, where $X_i = Q_i$, L_i, or K_i.

Turning next to another parameter of interest, the elasticity of substitution between labour and capital, this parameter is defined as:

$$\sigma = d \log(K_i / L_i) / d \log M \tag{8}$$

where the marginal rate of technical substitution, M, is given by

$$M = (\partial Q_i / \partial L_i) / (\partial Q_i / \partial K_i) \tag{9}$$

therefore, substituting (4) and (5) into (9) gives

$$M = (\beta_1 / \beta_2) (L_i / K_i)^{\lambda - 1} \tag{10}$$

hence, σ for this production function is given by

$$\sigma = 1 / (1 - \lambda) \tag{11}$$

Thus, it is clear from (11) that

$$\sigma \geq 0 \text{ as } \lambda \leq 1$$

and

$$\sigma < 0 \text{ as } \lambda > 1$$

Consequently, as long as the functional form is restricted to values of lambda not greater than unity, equation (1) is a CES production function. It is clear that in this model the elasticity of substitution, σ, depends upon the value of lambda obtained from the data used for estimation purposes. For example, if the estimated lambda is equal to zero, then σ is equal to unity and, therefore, the Cobb-Douglas production function (equation (2)) is the correct model.

Finally, turning to the main parameter of interest, namely, the total scale elasticity, ε_i:

$$\varepsilon_i = \Sigma (\partial Q_i / \partial X_i) (X_i / Q_i) \tag{12}$$

where, in the two input case, $X_i = L_i$ or K_i. For the CES production function used here, ε_i, is given by:

$$\varepsilon_i = \varepsilon_{Li} + \varepsilon_{Ki} \tag{13}$$

where $\varepsilon_{Li} = \beta_1 (Q_i / L_i)^{-\lambda}$ and $\varepsilon_{Ki} = \beta_2 (Q_i / K_i)^{-\lambda}$

Therefore, since equation (1) is non-homogeneous, the total scale elasticity, as expected, is variable (see Chapter 1) and depends upon the labour and capital productivity levels which are not constant. It is also clear from equation (13) that $(\partial \varepsilon_i / \partial z_i) \gtrless 0$, where $z_i = (Q_i / L_i)$ or $z_i = (Q_i / K_i)$, as $\lambda \gtrless 0$. For $\lambda < 0$ ($\sigma < 1$), ε_i increases as labour and capital productivities increase, while for $1 > \lambda > 0$ ($\sigma > 1$), ε_i decreases as productivities increase. It is also clear that for $\lambda = 0$ (equation (2), the Cobb-Douglas), the function is homogeneous and the degree of homogeneity is $\varepsilon_i = \beta_1 + \beta_2$ and, hence $(\partial \varepsilon_i / \partial z_i) = 0$.

Last but not least, turning to the estimation of equation (1), adding an error term, e_i, to the equation gives the specification used for estimation purposes. To estimate such an equation using maximum-likelihood, it is generally assumed that the error term is normally distributed. Unfortunately, the Box-Cox transformation approach implies that the distribution of e_i is truncated and, therefore, it cannot be normally distributed unless $\lambda = 0$ (see, *inter alia*, Fomby *et al.* (1984) and Amemiya (1985)). To proceed with maximum likelihood estimation here it will be assumed that truncation effects are negligible and the e_i are approximately independently identically distributed random variables with zero mean and constant variance. Under these assumptions the appropriate log of likelihood function is defined as:

$$\text{LLF} = \text{const} - (n/2) \ln\sigma^2 - (1/2) \sigma^2 (e'e) + (\lambda-1) \Sigma \ln Q \quad (14)$$

and since $\sigma^2 = (e'e)/n$, (14) can be respecified as the following LLF:

$$\text{LLF} = \text{const} - (n/2) \ln\sigma^2 + (\lambda-1) \Sigma \ln Q \quad (14a)$$

In this study equation (14)/(14a) is maximised using the procedures in Shazam (White (1978)). However, it is worthwhile to emphasise that, because e_i cannot be in reality normally distributed, equation (14)/(14a) should be regarded simply, as a 'maximard' that defines an 'extremum' estimator rather than a proper likelihood function.[25]

III. THE DATA

The data used for estimation purposes are cross-section statistics for the financial year July 1, 1983 through June 30, 1984. They cover observations of 33 *non-profit* county correction institutions (jails) in the

---

[25] This suggests that one cannot appeal to the theorem about the consistency of the maximum likelihood estimator; instead one must evaluate the probability limit at the value of parameters at which LLF is maximised. The results presented in this paper, therefore, must be interpreted in this light.

State of Tennessee, U.S.A. The output and input data employed were initially compiled and used by Hayes and Millar (1990) and are later reported in Mensah and Li (1993), Appendix. Output (Q_i) is measured as a number of jail days, where jail days is the sum of daily inmate population over the period under consideration. The (annual) number of employees is the measure used for labour (L_i). The possible capital stock (K_i) proxies that were available, and hence, could be used here were: the bed capacity and the physical space (in sq. ft.) of each jail. Here, the authors employed the physical space available at each jail, and not the bed capacity, as the better proxy for K_i. This is mainly because when the percentage of beds occupied is high (which is the case in all jails), the bed capacity proxy is perfectly correlated with the proxy for output-number of jail days.[25]

It should be emphasised, therefore, that these statistics are not reliable. Measurement errors, especially in capital stock statistics, are very likely. However, it should be also emphasised that the data used show wide variations across 33 units under consideration, consequently, minor inaccuracies are hopefully of little significance. Last but not least, it is important to point out that all the variables that will be used in this study are measured in *physical* units (see above) and not in *monetary* units (such as the values of output and capital). Consequently, the production function estimates that will be reported in the next section are 'engineering' production functions that define the technology (see Bairam (1994)) and, hence, unlike most previous studies in accounting and economics, they are mainly independent of the market structure (profit versus non-profit, competitive versus non-competitive settings etc.).

IV. THE RESULTS

Since four units are much larger than the other units in the data set,[27] preliminary estimates of equation (1) showed that the following specification, with two intercept dummies, is the most appropriate.[28]

---

[26] However, it is important to emphasise that since the two proxies discussed are highly correlated, the results reported in the next section do not qualitatively change if capital measure used is the bed capacity and not space available.

[27] See the bed capacity measures in Table 3.2 and Appendix 3.1 and the discussion Mensah and Li (1993), p. 81.

[28] Not reported here but can be obtained from the authors on request.

Table 3.1
Non-Homogeneous CES Production Function Estimates

No Estimates	(1)	(2)	(3)
α_0	5.54×10^2	1.61×10^2	4.72
	(0.91)*	(1.00)*	(1.70)*
α_1	-4.19×10^4	-1.72×10^5	-0.99
	(-4.23)	(-5.16)	(-1.19)*
α_2	-1.36×10^4	-4.47×10^4	-0.72
	(-4.22)	(-4.96)*	(-1.21)*
β_1	5.94×10^2	1.29×10^3	0.80
	(13.00)	(17.04)	(3.57)
β_2	1.04	1.25	0.39
	(4.90)	(5.66)	(2.75)
R^2	0.992	0.995	0.825
LLF	-329.75	-329.86	-338.64
$-2\log\theta$		0.22	13.78
λ	0.89	1.00	0.00
ε	1.34	1.34	1.19

Data Source: Mensah and Li (1993), Appendix (obtained from R.D. Hayes, coauthor Hayes and Millar (1990)).

Notes: R^2 and LLF are adjusted coefficient of determination and the log of the likelihood function, respectively. $-2\log\theta$ is the appropriate likelihood ratio used to test the hypothesis $\lambda = 1$ (the Leontief) and $\lambda = 0$ (the Cobb-Douglas). Given $-2\log\theta = -2$ [LLF ($\lambda = 1$ or $\lambda = 0$) - LLF(λ...)] is asymptotically distributed as χ^2 with one degree of freedom, if $\chi^2_{0.05} = 3.84 < -2\log\theta$, the Leontief or the Cobb-Douglas hypothesis is rejected (i.e., the CES hypothesis, H_1 is accepted). ε is the average scale elasticity for the 33 units under consideration. Finally the asymptotic t-statistics are shown in parenthesis (* denotes an estimated parameter not statistically significantly different from zero at the 0.05 test level).

$$f(Q_i) = \alpha_0 + \alpha_1 D_{1i} + \alpha_2 D_{2i} + \beta_1 f(L_i) + \beta_2 f(K_i) \tag{15}$$

where $D_1 = 1$ if unit 1 or 2 in the data set (largest two) and
$D_1 = 0$ if otherwise

$D_2 = 1$ if units 3 or 4 (3rd & 4th largest) and
$D_2 = 0$ if otherwise

all the variables are as before.

The estimated parameters obtained from equation (15) and its restricted versions ($\lambda = 1$ and $\lambda = 0$) are reported in Table 3.1. It is clear from the appropriate likelihood ratio test results reported ($-2\log\theta = 13.78$) that the correct λ value is statistically significantly different from zero at the conventional test levels. Consequently, this suggests that the Cobb-Douglas production function (Section II, equation (2)) which restricts lambda to zero (i.e. $\sigma = 1$) is not a good approximation for the functional form. Hence, the homogeneous (constant scale elasticity) production function does not define the technology used in the Tennessee prison system. On the other hand, the hypothesis $\lambda = 1$ cannot be rejected by the computed likelihood ratio ($-2\log\theta = 0.22$) reported in Table 3.1. This suggests that the linear Leontief production function (i.e. $\sigma = 0$) cannot be rejected. Therefore, it implies that capital-labour substitution is impossible in this industry, hence, the prison authorities cannot substitute labour with capital and vice versa to reduce cost of production when input prices change. This result clearly raises questions about appropriateness of cost functions in studying this non-competitive industry as the duality theory is suspect.[29]

Turning to the total scale elasticity (ε_i) which is the main parameter under consideration here, since the CES production function estimated is not homogeneous (i.e. since $\lambda \neq 0$), ε_i variable. Based on parameter estimates reported in Table 3.1, equation (1), the labour and capital estimates (ε_{Li} and ε_{Ki}), as well as total scale elasticities, for the 33 units were computed and are reported in Appendix 3.1. It is clear from these results that ε_i values vary from unit to unit but, from these results it is also clear that the largest and smallest units (1-5 and 25-33, respectively) are the most efficient, as in all these units increasing returns to scale prevails. On the other hand, for units with bed-capacity 37-99, degree of returns to scale are less predictable, i.e., depending upon the unit, decreasing, constant or increasing returns to scale are all possible.

---

[29] This will be reinforced below when total scale elasticity results in this study are compared with the estimates from Hayes and Millar (1990) and Mensah and Li (1993).

Table 3.2
Estimated Average Scale Elasticities: A Comparative Study

Size:		Nonhomog-eneous CES Production Function	Translog Cost Function: All Data	Translog Cost Function: Units 5-33	DEA: All Data	DEA: Units 5-33
Units	Bed Capacity					
1-4	633	IRTS	DRTS		DRTS	
5-10	93	DRTS	IRTS	IRTS	DRTS	DRTS
11-16	70	IRTS	IRTS	C/DRTS	IRTS	IRTS
17-22	55	CRTS	IRTS	DRTS	IRTS	IRTS
23-28	35	IRTS	IRTS	IRTS	IRTS	IRTS
29-33	14	IRTS	IRTS	IRTS	IRTS	IRTS

Sources: Appendix 3.1 and Mensah and Li (1993), Table 4.

Note: DRTS, CRTS and IRTS are decreasing, constant and increasing returns to scale, respectively.

Turning to comparison of the ε_i estimates with those obtained for the same units using data envelopment analysis (DEA) and a Translog cost function (Hayes and Millar (1990) and Mensah and Li (1993)), the average estimates from the three studies are summarised in Table 3.2. It is clear from these results that the ε_i estimates for small units are qualitatively the same from all three studies, namely, increasing returns to scale prevail in small units. On the other hand, ε_i estimates for very large and medium bed-capacity ones (units 1-4 and 5-10), are different quantitatively as well as qualitatively in the three studies.

This inconsistency from ε_i estimates, obtained from the production and cost functions for medium and large units, is no surprise to the present authors, as they confirm the unreliability of the duality theorem for non-competitive industries.

Both accounting and economics researchers should be very careful when they use cost functions instead of production functions as they may obtain inconsistent results. The present authors believe that the results from production and cost studies may not provide the same policy implications unless the study is for a competitive industry.

Furthermore, they believe, if the data are available, such studies should be a two-step procedure: first estimate physical production function (i.e. engineering production function), and, then, given this technical information, and factor input prices (and objectives) try to minimize these costs. The information gained this way, then, can be used in budgeting/planning, performance evaluation and monitoring/controlling processes. Unfortunately, both accounting and economics researchers, because of lack of data, avoid production functions in general, and physical production functions (i.e. engineering production function) in particular and estimate cost functions by employing the duality theory even when it is not appropriate.

V. CONCLUSIONS

The main objective of this study is to show that, in accounting and economics, the duality theorem may not work. For this purpose Hayes and Millar (1990) prison data were used and direct estimates from technical/engineering production functions obtained.

The results conclusively show that when an industry (like prisons) is non-competitive, the differing results from production functions and cost functions may not provide the same policy implications. Unfortunately, both in accounting and economics mainly due to lack of data, researchers have ignored production functions in general and physical engineering production functions in particular.

Appendix 3.1

Unit	Size	ε_{Ki}	ε_{Li}	ε_i	RTS
1	1244	0.23	1.20	1.43	IRTS
2	782	0.38	1.22	1.60	IRTS
3	292	0.47	0.94	1.41	IRTS
4	212	0.19	1.47	1.66	IRTS
5	108	0.59	0.52	1.10	IRTS
6	99	0.27	0.61	0.87	DRTS
7	99	0.17	0.43	0.60	DRTS
8	93	0.35	0.86	1.21	IRTS
9	86	0.17	0.80	0.97	CRTS
10	73	0.25	0.33	0.58	DRTS
11	72	0.83	1.10	1.93	IRTS
12	72	0.26	0.52	0.78	DRTS
13	71	0.20	0.45	0.65	DRTS
14	70	0.15	0.47	0.62	DRTS
15	68	0.46	1.10	1.57	IRTS
16	68	0.27	0.93	1.20	IRTS
17	66	0.13	0.55	0.68	DRTS
18	64	0.22	0.44	0.66	DRTS
19	58	0.53	0.59	1.12	IRTS
20	53	0.35	0.68	1.04	CRTS
21	48	0.45	0.74	1.19	IRTS
22	42	0.34	0.84	1.19	IRTS
23	42	0.31	1.11	1.42	IRTS
24	37	0.30	0.50	0.80	DRTS
25	37	0.39	0.92	1.31	IRTS
26	35	0.43	0.83	1.26	IRTS
27	28	0.54	0.53	1.07	IRTS
28	28	0.22	1.00	1.22	IRTS
29	22	0.19	1.17	1.35	IRTS
30	18	1.20	1.07	2.28	IRTS
31	16	0.47	0.86	1.33	IRTS
32	10	0.24	1.95	2.19	IRTS
33	6	1.10	3.29	4.34	IRTS

Sources: Table 3.1 and Mensah and Li (1993).
Note: Size is measured by the bed capacity. For the definition of ε_{Li}, ε_{Ki} and ε_i see section II. DRTS, CRTS and IRTS are decreasing, constant and increasing returns to scale, respectively.

REFERENCES

Amemiya, T. (1985), *Advanced Econometrics*, Harvard University Press, Cambridge, Mass.

Arrow *et al.* (1961), Capital-Labour Substitution and Economic Efficiency, *Review of Economics and Statistics*, 43, pp. 225-250.

Bairam, E.I. (1991a), Functional Form and New Production Functions: Some Comments and a New Variable Elasticity of Substitution Function, *Applied Economics*, 23, pp. 1247-1250.

Bairam, E.I. (1991b), Elasticity of Substitution, Technical Progress and Returns to Scale: A New CES Production Function Approach, *Journal of Applied Econometrics*, 6, pp. 91-96.

Bairam, E.I. (1994), *Homogeneous and Non-homogeneous Production Functions: Theory and Applications*, Avebury, Aldershot.

Box, G.E.P. and Cox, D.R. (1964), An Analysis of Transformations, *Journal of Royal Statistical Society*, Series B, 26, pp. 211-252.

Fomby, T.B., Hill, R. and Johnson, S. (1984), *Advanced Econometric Methods*, Springer-Verlag, New York.

Hayes, R.D. and Millar, J.A. (1990), Measuring Production Efficiency in a Non-for-profit Setting, *Accounting Review*, 65, pp. 505-519.

Hayes, R.D. and Millar, J.A. (1993), A Rejoinder to Measuring Production Efficiency in a Not-For-Profit Setting: An Extension, *Accounting Review*, 68, pp. 89-92.

Mensah, Y.M. and Li, S. (1993), Measuring Production Efficiency in a Not-for-profit Setting: An Extension, *Accounting Review*, 68, pp. 66-88.

Shephard R.W. (1970), *Theory of Cost and Production Functions*, Princeton University Press, Princeton, N.J.

Uzawa, H. (1964), Duality Principles in the Theory of Cost and Production, *International Economic Review*, 5, pp. 216-220.

White, K.J. (1978), A General Computer Program for Econometric Methods - Shazam, *Econometrica*, 46, pp. 239-240.

4 The Box-Cox Transformation as a VES Production Function

Murat Genç and
Erkin I. Bairam

I. INTRODUCTION

Ever since the introduction of the standard CES production function by Arrow, Chenery, Minhas and Solow (Arrow *et al.*, (1961)), researchers have developed numerous flexible functional forms that allow substitution between inputs to be unrestricted. Naturally, overwhelming attention was given to the functional forms that were linear in parameters. It is, however, not surprising that with the development of easy-to-use software, some attention has been given to nonlinear models lately.

One of these recent attempts, Bairam (1991b), after having suggested that the extended Box-Cox model can be interpreted as CES production function, suggests using a 'double' Box-Cox transformation to obtain variable elasticity of substitution between the inputs. The purpose of this short paper is to point out that just using a different transformation for each input in the extended Box-Cox model will suffice to obtain variable elasticity of substitution. The paper includes an application where elasticities of scale and substitution are estimated by using the extended Box-Cox model for a number of OECD countries.

II. THE EXTENDED BOX-COX MODEL AS A VES PRODUCTION FUNCTION

Bairam (1989, 1991a, 1991b) has shown that the extended Box-Cox model,

$$\frac{(y^\lambda - 1)}{\lambda} = A + \alpha \left[\frac{(x_1^\lambda - 1)}{\lambda}\right] + \beta \left[\frac{(x_2^\lambda - 1)}{\lambda}\right], \alpha, \beta > 0 \quad (1)$$

can be interpreted as a CES production function, provided that $\lambda \leq 1$. This is based on the observation that the production function $y = f(x_1, x_2)$ defined by the above specification has the following properties: (i) positive marginal productivities, (ii) quasi-concave for $\lambda \leq 1$, and (iii) constant elasticity of substitution, which can be shown to be $\sigma = \frac{1}{1-\lambda}$.

As Bairam argues, the advantage of this approach is that it allows us to estimate the elasticity of substitution without *a priori* assumptions about the functional form of the production function. The exact functional form of the production function is determined by the value of λ, which is an estimated parameter of the model. For example, $\lambda = 0$ corresponds to the Cobb-Douglas case.

Furthermore, as pointed out by Grimes (1991), equation (1) can be rewritten as

$$y = (\alpha + \beta)^{\frac{1}{\lambda}} \left[\frac{\lambda A + 1 - \alpha - \beta}{\alpha + \beta} + \frac{\alpha}{\alpha + \beta} x_1^\lambda + \frac{\beta}{\alpha + \beta} x_2^\lambda \right]^{\frac{1}{\lambda}}. \quad (2)$$

The implication is that the standard CES production function introduced by Arrow *et al.* (1961) – henceforth ACMS,

$$y = \gamma \left(ax_1^\lambda + bx_2^\lambda \right)^{\frac{1}{\lambda}}, \lambda < 1, \gamma > 0, \text{ and } 0 < a < 1, 0 < b < 1, \quad (3)$$

is, in fact, a special case of the extended Box-Cox model. The fact that the extended Box-Cox model is not homogeneous unless $\lambda A + 1 - \alpha - \beta = 0$, the case when it collapses to ACMS, is also appealing as homogeneity is quite a restrictive maintained hypothesis to employ.

Given this intepretation of the extended Box-Cox model, Bairam (1991a) then considers the following 'double' Box-Cox transformation:

$$\left[\left(\left(y^\lambda - 1 \right) / \lambda \right)^\phi - 1 \right) / \phi \right] = A + \alpha \left[\left(\left(x_1^\lambda - 1 \right) / \lambda \right)^\phi - 1 \right) / \phi \right]$$
$$+ \beta \left[\left(\left(x_2^\lambda - 1 \right) / \lambda \right)^\phi - 1 \right) / \phi \right], 1 < \lambda, \alpha, \beta > 0. \quad (4)$$

He argues that this is a VES production function, provided that $\phi \neq 1$ and $\lambda \neq 0$.

It is, however, unnecessary to apply a double transformation to obtain a variable elasticity of substitution. It is sufficient to let the variables in the extended Box-Cox model have a different transformation. That is, consider the specification

$$\frac{(y^{\lambda_0}-1)}{\lambda_0} = \alpha_0 + \alpha_1 \frac{(x_1^{\lambda_1}-1)}{\lambda_1} + \alpha_2 \frac{(x_2^{\lambda_2}-1)}{\lambda_2}, \ \alpha_i > 0. \quad (5)$$

The marginal productivity of inputs, $f_i = \frac{\partial y}{\partial x_i}$, can be obtained as

$$f_i = \alpha_i y^{1-\lambda_0} x_i^{\lambda_i-1} > 0, \ i = 1, 2. \quad (6)$$

It can also be shown that the determinant of the bordered Hessian of the production function is

$$H = -\alpha_1 \alpha_2 y^{3-3\lambda_0} x_1^{\lambda_1-2} x_2^{\lambda_2-2} \left[\alpha_1 x_1^{\lambda_1}(\lambda_2-1) + \alpha_2 x_2^{\lambda_2}(\lambda_1-1) \right]. \quad (7)$$

Thus, the production function defined by equation (5) will be quasi-concave if $\lambda_1 \leq 1$ and $\lambda_2 \leq 1$. This, together with positive marginal productivities of the inputs, allows us to interpret the given specification as a production function, provided that $\lambda_1 \leq 1$ and $\lambda_2 \leq 1$.

We can now evaluate the expression

$$\sigma = \frac{f_1 f_2 (f_1 x_1 + f_2 x_2)}{x_1 x_2 H}$$

to compute the elasticity of substitution between the inputs. This results in

$$\sigma = -\frac{\alpha_1 x_1^{\lambda_1} + \alpha_2 x_2^{\lambda_2}}{\alpha_1 x_1^{\lambda_1}(\lambda_2-1) + \alpha_2 x_2^{\lambda_2}(\lambda_1-1)}. \quad (8)$$

It is clear from this expression that σ is not constant so long as $\lambda_1 \neq \lambda_2$. Equation (5) can, therefore, be interpreted as a VES production function. When $\lambda_1 = \lambda_2$, equation (5) gives the CES case, of which Cobb-Douglas is a special case with $\lambda_1 = \lambda_2 = 0$.

We can also compute the elasticity of scale as

$$\varepsilon = \sum_i f_i \frac{x_i}{y} = \left(\alpha_1 x_1^{\lambda_1} + \alpha_2 x_2^{\lambda_2} \right) y^{-\lambda_0} \quad (9)$$

which is also variable.

III. AN APPLICATION: ELASTICITIES OF SUBSTITUTION AND SCALE IN OECD COUNTRIES

The main objective of this paper, so far, has been to point out that the extended Box-Cox model can be interpreted as a VES production function. We now demonstrate how and why the extended Box-Cox model should be used by estimating an aggregate production function based on aggregate pooled cross-country data from a selection of OECD countries.[30]

Taking equation (5) and adding an error term, u, gives the following specification for estimation purposes:

$$\frac{(y^{\lambda_0}-1)}{\lambda_0} = \alpha_0 + \alpha_1 \frac{(x_1^{\lambda_1}-1)}{\lambda_1} + \alpha_2 \frac{(x_2^{\lambda_2}-1)}{\lambda_2} + u \qquad (5a)$$

where y is output, and x_1 and x_2 are capital and labour. Capital is measured as the physical capital stock and labour as the total number of workers.

For the purposes of converting the output (which is measured as GDP) and capital stock to a constant price-common currency (US dollars), GDP price indices and exchange rates were used. It is also worthwhile to emphasise that capital stock was adjusted for capacity utilisation. However, unfortunately, the labour measure used here can deviate from labour services as changes in working hours, underemployment, etc. can cause a problem. Fortunately, despite this problem, x_2 shows wide variations among the relevant countries under consideration. Therefore, minor inaccuracies are, hopefully, of little significance. Nevertheless, the estimated equations reported and discussed below must be interpreted in this light.

The maximum likelihood estimation of equation (5a) requires the assumption of normality of the error term u. Due to the nature of the data used here, this is a more realistic assumption than most other data

---

[30] The data we use are from Hansen and Knowles (1995) and can be obtained from the present authors. The data are constructed for years 1965, 1970, 1975, 1980 and 1985.

Table 4.1

The VES Production Function Estimates, 1965-85

α_0	α_1	α_2	λ_0	λ_1	λ_2	LLF	R^2	LRT (χ_r^2)
0.290 (0.66)*	0.501 (8.59)	0.600 (13.00)	0.00	0.00	0.00	-676.51	0.976	9.30 (r=3)
0.762 (3.17)	0.515 (7.26)	0.347 (14.06)	-0.19	-0.19	-0.19	-675.09	0.977	6.46 (r=2)
-8.862 (-9.26)	0.796 × 10⁻³ (11.13)	5.528 (18.92)	-0.02	0.45	-0.26	-671.86	0.980	–

Source: Hansen and Knowles (1995).

Notes: The asymptotic t-statistics are shown in parenthesis; (*) denotes an α coefficient not significantly different from zero at the 5% test. LRT is the appropriate likelihood ratio test used to test the hypothesis $H_0 : \lambda_0 = \lambda_1 = \lambda_2$ (or $H_0 : \lambda_0 = \lambda_1 = 0$). They are asymptotically distributed as χ^2 with r degrees of freedom.

series used in other studies which use Box-Cox and maximum likelihood for estimation purposes.[31]

Equation (5a) is estimated using the combined Box-Cox and Box-Tidwell maximum likelihood approach in Shazam (White (1978)) which assumes that all the variables (y, x_1 and x_2) in the specification have different lambda values (λ_0, λ_1, and λ_2). We have also estimated the two restricted versions of equation (5a) (with $\lambda_0 = \lambda_1 = \lambda_2$, the CES case, and with $\lambda_0 = \lambda_1 = \lambda_2 = 0$, the Cobb-Douglas case) using the extended Box-Cox model in Shazam.

The estimated three equations are presented in Table 4.1.[32] These results and the two likelihood test statistics computed ($\chi_2^2 = 6.46$ and $\chi_3^2 = 9.30$) to test the hypotheses $H_0 : \lambda_0 = \lambda_1 = \lambda_2$ (the CES) and $H_0 : \lambda_0 = \lambda_1 = \lambda_2 = 0$ (the Cobb-Douglas) reveal that both the CES and the Cobb-Douglas specifications are inappropriate. This suggests that the unrestricted specification in equation (5a) is the appropriate production function.

Consequently, the variable elasticity of substitution between labour and capital, σ_{it}, where i = country and t = year, the variable scale elasticity of capital ε_{1it}, and that of labour, ε_{2it}, as well as the total scale elasticity ($\varepsilon_{1it} + \varepsilon_{2it} = \varepsilon_{it}$) were calculated using the statistically significant α parameters in the third estimated equation. These results are reported in Table 4.2.

Turning to a brief interpretation of these elasticities for the eleven countries under consideration, it is clear that all scale elasticities reported vary from country to country and from period to period. Average scale elasticity for capital is 0.45 and for labour is 0.66, adding up to 1.11 and suggesting some economies of scale. However, the total scale elasticities for individual countries range from 0.75 in 1965 for Japan (i.e., large diseconomies of scale) to 1.49 in 1985 for the USA (large economies of scale). Furthermore, it is worthwhile to note that most of the variation in total elasticity of scale, ε_{it}, is attributable to the increase in the scale elasticity of capital and not to changes in the scale elasticity of labour.

Finally, the reported results show that the estimated elasticities of substitution between the inputs, σ_{it}, are very elastic. The average elasticity of substitution for eleven countries for the periods under

---

[31] This is mainly because, given that Box-Cox transformation cannot handle non-positive values, it is likely that the researchers would end up with truncated samples. However, since y, x_1 and x_2 are all positive here, this is not a problem.

[32] It is worthwhile to note that we have initially included a time trend variable in our estimation. The results revealed that this variable was not statistically significant.

Table 4.2

Variable Scale Elasticities (ε_{it}) and Elasticities of Substitution (σ_{it}) by Country and by Period

Country	Year	ε_{1it}	ε_{2it}	ε_{it}	σ_{it}
Austria	1965	0.31	0.77	1.08	1.71
	1985	0.38	0.70	1.08	1.70
Belgium	1965	0.20	0.81	1.01	1.74
	1985	0.26	0.82	1.08	1.73
Canada	1965	0.30	0.70	1.00	1.72
	1985	0.41	0.62	1.03	1.69
Finland	1965	0.20	0.92	1.12	1.74
	1985	0.22	0.90	1.12	1.74
France	1965	0.35	0.54	0.89	1.71
	1985	0.57	0.53	1.10	1.65
West Germany	1965	0.42	0.49	0.91	1.69
	1985	0.66	0.51	1.17	1.63
Japan	1965	0.33	0.42	0.75	1.71
	1985	0.68	0.41	1.09	1.63
Norway	1965	0.19	1.01	1.20	1.74
	1985	0.24	0.97	1.21	1.73
Sweden	1965	0.34	0.81	1.15	1.70
	1985	0.40	0.78	1.18	1.69
U.K.	1965	0.66	0.52	1.18	1.63
	1985	0.60	0.51	1.11	1.64
U.S.A.	1965	0.89	0.38	1.28	1.58
	1985	1.14	0.35	1.49	1.53
Belgium	1965	0.20	0.81	1.01	1.74
	1985	0.26	0.82	1.08	1.73
Averages		0.45	0.66	1.11	1.68
Range		0.95	0.55	0.74	0.21

Sources: Table 4.1 and Hansen and Knowles (1995).
Notes: Averages are calculated from the pooled estimates for 1965, 1970, 1975, 1980 and 1985.

consideration is 1.68. However, it is still statistically significantly different from country to country but the range is small, 0.20.

Therefore, summing it up, the above results show that both the elasticity of substitution and the total scale elasticity are variable and imposing *a priori* assumptions on the estimated production function is unrealistic. This has important implications and consequences for applied production function literature and eventually for economic theory.

V. CONCLUSION

We have shown that the extended Box-Cox model with different transformations of the variables can be interpreted as a VES production function, provided that both λ_1 and λ_2 are less than or equal to one. The use of equation (5) in econometric analysis of the technology places no *a priori* assumptions about the production function. This specification is not only flexible in this sense but also lets the data determine the exact functional form of the production function. Once the model is estimated, the assumption of constancy of substitution can explicitly be tested in a straightforward fashion. The model also yields simple formulae to compute the variable elasticities of substitution and scale.

REFERENCES

Arrow, K., Chenery, H.B., Minhas, B. and Solow, R.M. (1961), Capital-labour substitution and economic efficiency, *Review of Economics and Statistics*, 43, pp. 225-250.

Bairam, E. (1989), Functional form and the elasticity of substitution: a new CES production function, *Economic Discussion Papers*, No. 8904, University of Otago, New Zealand.

Bairam, E. (1991a), Functional form and new production functions: some comments and a new VES function, *Applied Economics*, 23, pp. 1247-1250.

Bairam, E. (1991b), Elasticity of substitution, technical progress and returns to scale in branches of Soviet industry: a new CES production function approach, *Journal of Applied Econometrics*, 6, pp. 91-96.

Grimes, A. (1991), A new production function? Bowled by a googly, *Applied Economics*, 23, pp. 1245-1246.

Hansen, P. and Knowles, S. (1995), Returns to scale in an aggregate production function that includes human capital, *Economic Discussion Papers*, No. 9503, University of Otago, New Zealand.

White, K.T. (1978), A general computer program for econometric methods - Shazam, *Econometrica*, 46.

5 The Form of Production Function for the Chinese Regional Economy

Erkin I. Bairam

I. INTRODUCTION

This paper is mainly concerned with estimating appropriate production functions for the Chinese economy using provincial data, 1973-89. It is hoped that the results obtained would help to assess the variabilities in the scale elasticity, elasticity of substitution and technical progress over time. It is hoped also that the results obtained would help to assess the roles of economies of scale, elasticity of substitution and technical progress in Chinese economic growth.[33]

The outline of the paper is as follows: In Section II the basic model used for estimation purposes is discussed. Section III discusses the estimation procedures used, results obtained and assesses their technical and economic implications. Finally Section IV summarizes the main conclusions to be drawn from the paper.

II. THE CONSTANT MARGINAL SHARE (CMS) PRODUCTION FUNCTION

In his study of factor contribution to growth in the Israeli economy, where neither the labour nor the capital markets could be assumed to be in equilibrium, Bruno (1968), introduced the following production function which is discussed, in detail, in Chapter 1:

$$Q_t = A(e^{\lambda t}) L_t^{\alpha} K_t^{\beta} - \gamma L_t \tag{1}$$

---

[33] There are not many production function studies of the Chinese economy in particular at the disaggregate level. The recent ones which the present author knows are the following: Tidrick (1986), Chen *et al.* (1988), Jia (1991), Bairam (1994), Chapter 10.

It is shown in Chapter 1 that notwithstanding the fact that the labour scale elasticity is constant, because the capital scale elasticity is variable, the total scale elasticity is variable and is equal to:

$$\varepsilon = \alpha + \beta + [\beta \gamma (L_t/Q_t)] \qquad (2)$$

Finally, it is worthwhile to note that since the shift factor $Ae^{\lambda t}$ (level of technology at year t) only appears in the first term of the production function (ie the Cobb-Douglas component), technical progress (λ) will be neutral only asymptotically, as t becomes large. Otherwise its effect is to increase the marginal rate of technical substitution for any given (K_t/L_t) according to whether γ is positive or negative.[34]

III. ESTIMATION AND THE RESULTS

The data sets used for estimation purposes are from Tein-tung et al. (1993). They cover four Chinese provinces with complete data sets for the period 1973-89. It should be noted that the output, labour and capital stock data used may not be entirely reliable.[35] However, it should be also emphasised that the data used show wide variations over time, therefore, minor inaccuracies are hopefully of little significance. Nevertheless the results reported must be interpreted in this light.

Turning to the estimation of the CMS function, equation (1) was estimated by maximum likelihood procedures. However, the preliminary estimations of the function for the four provinces under consideration (Jiangsu, Inner Mongolia, Shanxi and Zhejiang) revealed that the disturbance terms are serially correlated (results are not reported). Consequently, the equations were re-estimated using the maximum likelihood procedure described in Pagan (1974) which corrected the estimated equations for first order serial correlation. The results are reported in Table 5.1.

---

[34] The case $\gamma > 0$ in which technical progress starts off being 'capital saving' (the marginal rule increases with t) is interesting. One way of looking at this might be that the labour force is undergoing some process of 'learning' with time in a way that increases their marginal product in relation to that of capital (see Bairam (1994) p. 43). This may very well be a more realistic description for an economy in early stages of rapid industrialisation than ordinary 'neutrality' assumption (ie $\gamma = 0$).

[35] This is mainly because from the input side there is a common tendency to assume that there are no significant variations in the degree of utilisation of inputs over time.

Table 5.1
The Production Function Estimates

Province	A	λ	α	β	γ	R^2	DW
1. Jiangsu	5.93 (3.67)	0.016 (5.65)	0.74 (15.06)	0.07 (1.14)*	1.33 (2.41)	0.994	1.49
2. Inner Mongolia	12.31 (5.99)	0.005 (15.76)	0.85 (44.96)	0.01 (0.30)*	4.47 (5.16)	0.967	1.87
3. Shanxi	0.94 (3.08)	0.002 (0.31)*	0.87 (4.08)	0.19 (1.75)	0.81 (1.89)	0.934	2.17
4. Zhejiang	1.11 (11.13)	0.009 (4.47)	0.93 (25.10)	0.14 (3.07)	1.01 (11.40)	0.994	1.69

Source: Tien-tung *et al.* (1993).

Notes: Figures in parentheses are asy. t-statistics. * indicates a coefficient not significantly different from zero at 0.05 (one tailed) test level. For other notes see text.

64

It is clear from these results that, at the 5 percent test level, the estimated γ values are significantly greater than zero in all four regions. Based on these reported γ values, it is clear that both the scale elasticity (ε_t) and the elasticity of substitution (σ_t) are variable. The estimated ε_t and σ_t values for all four regions, 1973-89, are reported in Appendix 5.1. It is clear from the results that, since $\gamma > 0$, as expected the elasticity of substitution is significantly less than unity in all regions and it is monotonically approaching 1 from below over time. This clearly suggests that although elasticity of substitution labour for capital is still difficult, (in particular in Shanxi and Zhejang) with economic development it will get relatively easy. Turning to the scale elasticity, ε_t, although it is variable it is not changing significantly over time in Jiangsu and Inner Mongolia simply because one of the coefficients effecting ε_t over time (β) is small **and** statistically insignificant (see equation (8)). However, even if ε_t is taken as constant in these two regions, the results suggest minor diseconomies of scale. On the other hand, as the estimated β coefficients for the other two regions (Shanxi and Zhejang) are significant (and relatively large) ε_t varies more in these two regions. It is clear from the appendix results that for Shanxi and Zhejang significant economies of scale prevail but are declining over time. Consequently, summing it up, the estimated ε_t values clearly show that the degree of returns to scale varies from region to region and, furthermore, to a lesser extent, with the same region over time.

Finally, turning to exogenous technical progress, λ, it can be seen from Table 5.1 it is very modest in all regions - varying from 0.02% per annum in Shanxi to 1.60% per annum in Jiangsu. This clearly shows that, compared with other developing countries (Bairam (1994)) technical progress does not play a major role in the regions of the Chinese economy under consideration. However, it is worthwhile to emphasise that, given $\gamma > 0$ for all the regions, it is very clear that the labour force in China is undergoing some process of learning with time. This confirms that the economy is in its early stages of rapid industrialisation and the rate of technical progress, although low, is not neutral.

IV. CONCLUSION

In this paper the constant marginal share production function is estimated using Chinese provincial time-series data, 1973-89.

The results obtained refute the *a priori* homogeneity assumption (ie the Cobb-Douglas). They suggest that the elasticity of substitution and the scale elasticity are variable and provincial differences in all the estimated parameters are very large.

Appendix 5.1

Scale Elasticities and Elasticities of Substitution by Province and by Year

Year	Jiangsu ε	σ	Inner Mongolia ε	σ	Shanxi ε	σ	Zherjiang ε	σ
1973	0.86	0.87	0.92	0.93	NA	NA	1.38	0.67
1974	0.87	0.88	0.92	0.93	NA	NA	1.47	0.57
1975	0.87	0.88	0.92	0.93	1.52	0.47	1.48	0.56
1976	0.87	0.88	0.92	0.93	1.61	0.37	1.80	0.54
1977	0.88	0.86	0.93	0.92	1.50	0.49	1.39	0.65
1978	0.87	0.88	0.93	0.92	1.43	0.59	1.39	0.66
1979	0.86	0.88	0.93	0.92	1.58	0.40	1.37	0.68
1980	0.86	0.89	0.93	0.91	1.48	0.51	1.36	0.69
1981	0.87	0.88	0.94	0.90	1.51	0.48	1.36	0.69
1982	0.86	0.89	0.94	0.90	1.48	0.51	1.35	0.70
1983	0.86	0.89	0.94	0.91	1.44	0.56	1.33	0.72
1984	0.85	0.90	0.93	0.92	1.42	0.58	1.29	0.75
1985	0.85	0.90	0.93	0.92	1.42	0.58	1.30	0.76
1986	0.85	0.91	0.93	0.92	1.43	0.57	1.29	0.77
1987	0.85	0.91	0.93	0.92	1.42	0.58	1.28	0.78
1988	0.84	0.91	0.93	0.92	1.43	0.57	1.28	0.77
1989	0.84	0.91	0.93	0.92	1.44	0.56	1.28	0.77

Sources: Tien-tung *et al.* (1993) and Table 1.

Notes: See text.

REFERENCES

Bairam, E.I. (1994), *Homogeneous and Nonhomogeneous Production Functions*, Avebury, Aldershot, UK and Brookfield, USA.

Bruno, M. (1968), Estimation of Factor Contribution to Growth under Structural Disequilibrium, *International Economic Review*, 9, pp. 49-62.

Chen, K., *et al.* (1988), Productivity Change in Chinese Industry: 1953-85, *Journal of Comparative Economics*, 12, pp. 570-91.

Jia, L. (1991), A Quantitative Analysis of Chinese Industrial Structure and Technological Change: Production Functions for Aggregate Industry, Sectoral Industries and Small Scale Industries, *Applied Economics*, 23, pp. 1733-40.

Pagan, A.R. (1974), A Generalized Approach to the Treatment of Autocorrelation, *Australian Economic Papers*, 13, pp. 267-280.

Tein-tung, H., *et al.* (1993), *China's Provincial Statistics, 1949-1988*, Westview Press, Boulder, USA and Oxford, UK.

Tidrick, G. (1986), Productivity Growth and Technical Change in Chinese Industry, *World Bank Staff Working Papers*, No. 761.

6 Linear versus Non-Linear Technical Progress and Production Functions: Theory and Some Evidence

Erkin I. Bairam

I. INTRODUCTION

Ever since Black (1962), showed that the linear technical progress function can be derived from a Cobb-Douglas production function, it has been surrounded by considerable controversy (see, for example, Bairam (1987)).

This paper is mainly concerned with discussing the theory and, for the first time, analysing the underlying structure and the appropriate shape of the technical progress function.

The outline of the paper is as follows. In Sections II(i) and III(i). the relevant theories are discussed and further developed. Sections II(ii). and III(ii) apply the models developed using cross-section data based on 107 countries and discuss the implications and the limitations of the results obtained. Finally Section IV concludes the paper.

II. THE COBB-DOUGLAS VERSUS NON-HOMOGENEOUS PRODUCTION FUNCTIONS AND LINEAR TECHNICAL PROGRESS

i) Theory

Over 30 years ago Black (1962) showed that linear specification of Kaldor's technical progress function (TPF, Kaldor (1957)), can be derived from the homogeneous Cobb-Douglas function:

$$Y = A(\tau) N^\alpha K^\beta \tag{1}$$

where Y, N, K are levels of output, labour and capital stock respectively and τ is the time trend. This function is homogeneous to the degree

$\alpha+\beta$ and $A(\tau)$ is the level of exogeneous technology available and used at time τ.

If it is assumed that constant returns to scale prevail (i.e. $\alpha = 1-\beta$), equation (1) can be rewritten as:

$$(Y/N) = A(\tau) (K/N)^\beta \tag{2}$$

Taking the natural log of equation (2) yields:

$$\ln(Y/N) = \ln A(\tau) + \beta \ln(K/N) \tag{3}$$

and differentiating (3) with respect to time gives the linear TPF:

$$(y-n) = a + \beta(k-n) \tag{4}$$

where lower case letters denote the growth rates of the relevant variables and $a = [\partial \ln A(\tau)/\partial \ln t]$ is the exogenous rate of technical progress. Hence it can be concluded that, if the constant returns to scale Cobb-Douglas production function is appropriate for a given economy, the linear TPF, which shows the relationship between the rates of growth of labour productivity (or per capita output) and capital-labour ratio (or per capita capital), can be derived from it.[36]

This clearly means that, the linear technical progress function would definitely yield results different from the appropriate production function, if and only if, the underlying production function is not the constant returns to scale Cobb-Douglas production function. Here in Section II(ii), this research, will explicitly test whether or not this is the case by specifying the relationship between (Y/N) and K/N) as a general Box-Cox model (see Bairam (1991, 1994), and Chapter 1):

$$\{[(Y/N)^\lambda -1]/\lambda\} = B(\tau) + \beta\{[(K/N)^\lambda -1]/\lambda\} \tag{5}$$

where $\infty^+ \geq \lambda \geq \infty^+$ $B(\tau), \beta \geq 0$

Therefore, unless $\lambda=0$, equation (5) yields non-homogeneous production functions which are CES (see Chapter 1). It is only when $\lambda=0$ equation (5) collapses to the linear homogenous Cobb-Douglas production function – i.e. to equation (3) with $B(\tau) = \ln A(\tau)$.[37] Hence,

---

[36] The linear and non-linear TPFs will be discussed in detail in Section 3.1 but, here it is worthwhile to mention that Dixon and Thirlwall (1975) derived the Verdoorn Law [see the review by Bairam (1987)] from the linear TPF (i.e. equation (4) above) and, therefore, the underlying structure of the Verdoorn Law may also be the Cobb-Douglas production function.

[37] This is because using L' Hospital's rule it can be shown that when $\lambda=0$, $[(X^\lambda -$

the linear TPF (equation (4)) can be derived from equation (5) if and only if $\lambda=0$. Thus, testing the Cobb-Douglas hypothesis is equivalent to testing whether or not $\lambda=0$.

Finally, before the above hypothesis is tested, as it will be useful later on, it is also worthwhile to examine one other important property of this general function. Equation (5) yields the following productivity (or per capita output) elasticity.

$$\begin{aligned}\varepsilon &= [\partial(Y/N)/\partial K/N)] \, [(K/N) \, (Y/N)] \\ &= \beta(Y/K)^\lambda \end{aligned} \qquad (6)$$

It is clear from equation (6) that the productivity level elasticity, ε, depends upon the values of λ, β and (Y/K). Therefore, since (Y/K) is likely to be variable over-time or across-units, unless $\lambda=0$, (i.e. the Cobb-Douglas), ε is not constant.[38]

Therefore, summing it up, unless $\lambda=0$ (i.e. unless the Cobb-Douglas is the correct model) the elasticity between per capita output and per capita capital is variant over time.

ii) Evidence

In this section equation (5) and its restricted version (i.e. equation (3), the Cobb-Douglas production function) will be estimated from cross-country data using the Box-Cox procedures in Shazam (White (1978)) computer programme. The data used for estimation purposes are from King and Levine (1994). This set which will be used here and in Section III(ii), covers 107 countries and includes the 1980s averages for the following critical variables: real GDP per capita (Y/N), capital stock per capita (K/N) and the inverse of capital output ratio (i.e. capital productivity level, (Y/K)).

Preliminary estimates of equation (5) with dummy variables as expected (see Bairam (1994)), revealed that the level of technical progress differs at different stages of economic development. Consequently $B(\tau)$ for equations (3) and (4) in Table 6.1(a), which used the full-sample (n=107), is specified as:

---

1) $/\lambda] = \ln X$, where $X = (Y/N)$ or (K/N).
[38] Furthermore, under the realistic assumption $\beta>0$, the direction of change in the elasticity, ε, is as follows:
$\quad [\partial\varepsilon/\partial(Y/K)] <0 \quad$ as $\lambda>0$
$\quad [\partial\varepsilon/\partial(Y/K)] >0 \quad$ as $\lambda<0$
$\quad [\partial\varepsilon/\partial(Y/K)] =0 \quad$ as $\lambda=0$

Table 6.1

The Relationship between Real GDP per Capita (Y/N) and Capital Stock per Capita (K/N), Cross-Country Data, Averages 1980s

(a) Full Sample (n = 107)

No.	β_0	β_1	β_2	β_3	β	λ	R^2	LLF	LRT
(1)	8.09				0.62	0.30	0.929	-867.50	
	(10.54)				(37.32)				
(2)	2.00				0.70	0	0.901	-881.52	26.06
	(10.40)				(31.13)				
(3)	29.81	6.01	-13.72	-7.35	0.43	0.35	0.953	-844.94	
	(9.09)	(2.99)	(-6.08)	(-4.90)	(13.53)				
(4)	4.25	0.25	-0.84	-0.40	0.50	0	0.939	-860.04	33.08
	(11.31)	(1.73)*	(-6.60)	(-4.57)	(13.76)				

(b) Sub-Sample (n = 47)

No.	β_0	β_1	β_2	β_3	β	λ	R^2	LLF	LRT
(1)	12.73				0.57	0.33	0.943	-391.89	
	(8.65)				(27.62)				
(2)	2.15				0.70	0	0.939	-397.58	12.62
	(8.76)				(26.65)				
(3)	48.28		-19.90	-11.87	0.38	0.41	0.956	-384.46	
	(6.74)		(-3.85)	(-3.94)	(8.87)				
(4)	3.74		-0.49	-0.29	0.55	0	0.951	-391.52	7.12
	(6.67)		(-2.96)	(-3.51)	(10.03)				

Data Source: King and Levine (1994).

Notes: For the specification of the equations, estimation procedures and the definition of the samples used see the text. Asym. t-values are shown in parentheses (* denotes the estimated coefficient not statistically significant at the conventional test levels. LLF is the log of the likelihood function and LRT is the appropriate likelihood ratio used to test the hypothesis: $H_0 : \lambda=0$ against $H_1 : \lambda \neq 0$. It is computed as follows: LRT = -2 [LLF($\lambda=0...$)]-LLF($\lambda \neq 0...$)] and asym. distributed as χ^2 with 1 degree of freedom. Therefore, if $\chi^2{}_{0.05} = 3.84 <$ LRT H_0 (i.e. the Cobb-Douglas hypothesis) is rejected.

$$B(\tau) = \beta_0 + \beta_1 O + B_2 D_2 + \beta_3 D_3$$

where O=1 if country i is an oil exporting country O=0 if otherwise, D_2=1 if country i had an average per capita income less than \$3,000US, D_2=0 if otherwise; and D_3=1 if the country had a per capita income in the 1980s between \$3,000 and \$6,000US, D_3=0 if otherwise.

This specification of $B(\tau)$ clearly implies that the level of technology is equal to β_0 in developed OECD countries, $(\beta_0 + \beta_3)$ in most fast-developing countries and $(\beta_0 + \beta_2)$ in the least developed countries. As can be seen from the results in Table 1(a), the evidence supports all the expected parameter signs, namely: $\beta_1>0$, β_2, $\beta_3<0$.

The statistical significance of the dummies clearly suggests that either equation (3) or (4) in Table 6.1(a) is the correct specification. Consequently, for the most of this section the focus will be on the two equations.

Now turning to finding the most appropriate specification of equation (5) for the full-sample of 107 countries, the validity of the restriction on λ (namely $\lambda=0$, the Cobb-Douglas) is tested using the appropriate likelihood ratio test results in Table 6.1(a). It is clear from the results the log-linear model is not the appropriate specification as the null H_0: $\lambda=0$ is rejected against the possible alternative $(H_1:\lambda=0)$. Therefore the estimated equations in Table 6.1(a) conclusively show that the constant returns to scale Cobb-Douglas is not the appropriate production function. Thus the linear TPF, if it is appropriate TPF, cannot be derived from the underlying appropriate production function.

It is also worthwhile to point out that this also clearly suggests that the elasticity, ε, which was derived and discussed in the previous section, is variable. The final estimates of ε reported in Appendix 6.1 show that their average value is 0.52 (very close to $\beta=0.50$ from equation (4) in Table 6.1(b), i.e. from the Cobb-Douglas specification) but it has a range of 0.43, varying from 0.27 to 0.70 and in general is lower (less than 0.5) in most, less developed countries.[39]

III. LINEAR VERSUS NON-LINEAR TECHNICAL PROGRESS FUNCTIONS

i) Theory

It is clear from the results reported in the previous section that the Cobb-Douglas production function cannot be the underlying structure

---

[39] For computational purposes equation (6) in the previous section and equation (3) in Table 6.1(a) were used.

for the linear TPF (equation (4)) simply because it is not the appropriate production function for the data under consideration. But does this mean that the linear TPF is still valid or does it mean the appropriate TPF is also non-linear and non-homogeneous? The author will try to answer this question in Section III(ii) but before he proceeds to that attempt, it is important and worthwhile to discuss the TPF further.

Kaldor (1957) specified his technical progress function as:

$$(y-n) = a+\beta f(k-n) \qquad (7)$$

where the variables are defined as before and f denotes the functional form (which linearity is a special case).

He argued that:
> *Some* increases in productivity would take place even if capital per man [K/N] remains constant over time, since there is always some innovation which enables production to be increased without additional investment. But beyond these, the growth in productivity [y/n] depends on the rate of growth of capital stock [k][40] though there is likely to be some maximum beyond which the rate of growth of productivity could not be raised, however, fast capital is being accumulated. Hence the [technical progress] curve is likely to be convex upwards and flatten out altogether beyond a certain point (Kaldor (1957), p.596).

Therefore Kaldor believed that:
(i) there exists exogeneous technical progress (i.e. a>0);
(ii) the function is not only non-linear, and has a first derivative with respect to (k-n) positive (i.e. f'>0), but, furthermore its second derivative is negative ($f''<0$).

Unfortunately, he himself respecified the TPF he used in his theoretical model (Kaldor(1957)) as linear, namely equation (4)[41]:

$$(y-n) = a+\beta(k-n)$$

This TPF is a function, therefore assumes f''=0 and, as shown in Section II(i) can be derived from a constant return to scale Cobb-Douglas production function. Hence, as emphasised before, this specification not only makes the TPF a more dynamic Cobb-Douglas production

---

[40] Throughout his discussion Kaldor assumes n=0 (or constant), hence, the growth rate in k is equal to growth rate in (K/N). Here this assumption would not be made.

[41] Indeed, as mentioned in the previous footnote, he further assumed that n=0 and, hence, the TPF function used was y=a+βk.

function but now it is clear that it also refutes Kaldor's own claim that f"<0.

It is clear from the discussion so far that three types of relationship between (y-n) and (k-n) are possible: f"=0, f">0 and f"<0. Unfortunately, so far in the literature the shape of the TPF has not been tested on any data set. Consequently, the sign of f" is not known.

Here in Section III(ii), the shape of the TPF will be explicitly tested using the following specification:

$$\{[(y-n)^\lambda - 1]/\lambda\} = b_0 + \beta\{[(k-n)^\lambda - 1]/\lambda\} \tag{8}$$

where $b_0, \beta \geq 0$ and $\infty^+ \geq \lambda \geq \infty^-$

It is obvious from this equation that the linear model (equation 4) is a special case of this general Box-Cox model (see Bairam (1994)). It is only when $\lambda=1$ that equation (8) collapses to the linear TPF. Hence, testing for the linear technical progress function is equivalent to testing whether or not $\lambda=1$.

This can also be shown from the first and second order derivatives. Differentiation (y-n) with respect to (k-n) yields:

$$f' = \beta[(k-n)/(y-n)]^{\lambda-1} > 0 \tag{9a}$$

and

$$f'' = \beta[(k-n/(y-n)]^\lambda - (k-n)^{-1}(1-\lambda)\{\beta[(k-n)/(y-n)]^\lambda - 1\} \gtreqless 0 \tag{9b}$$

Therefore, as long as $\beta>0$, f'>0 but the sign of f" could be postive, negative or zero, depending upon β, λ and $\{\beta[(k-n)/(y-n)]^\lambda - 1\}$, it is clear that if $\lambda=1$, as expected, $f'=\beta$ and f"=0.

ii) Evidence

This section starts with the estimation of the LTP using the same data briefly discussed in Section III(ii). The full sample size again is 107 observations and (y-n) and (k-n) are the average growth rates of GDP per capita and capital per capita in the 1980s, respectively.

In order to take into account that the exogeneous rate of technical progress, like the level of technical progress, could differ among the countries (in particular among the ones at different stages of their economic development), the linear technical progress function, equation (4), was respecified with the dummies also used in Section II(ii):

$$(y-n) = b_0 + b_1 O + b_2 D_2 + b_3 D_3 + \beta(k-n) \tag{4a}$$

Table 6.2(a)

The Linear Technical Progress Function
Full Sample (n=107), OLS Estimates
$(y=n) = b_0 + b_1 O + b_2 D_2 + b_3 D_3 + \beta(k-n)$

No.	b_0	b_1	b_2	b_3	β	R^2	BPG	RESET (4)
(1)	-0.001				0.37	0.234	10.84	11.60
	(-0.26)				(5.79)			
(2)	-0.007	-0.059	-0.009	-0.001	0.39	0.420	30.02	6.81
	(-1.82)*	(-5.80)	(-1.90)*	(-0.26)*	(6.73)			

Data Source: King and Levine (1994).

Notes: See the text for specification and estimation procedures. t-statistics are shown in parentheses (* denotes that the estimated coefficient is not statistically significantly different from zero at the 0.05 test level). BPG is the Breuch, Pagan and Godfrey heteroscedasticity test (with a critical $\chi^2_{0.05}$ value of 9.49) and RESET(4) is the fourth power RESET specification test (with a critical $F_{0.05}$ value of 2.68).

All the variables and the dummies are as before and the dummies were discussed in Section II(ii).

Equation (4) and (4a) were estimated by OLS. The results are reported in Table 6.2(a). As can be seen from these results, the only significant dummy is the oil export dummy and it has a negative sign, $b_1<0$. However, both equations in this table (equations (1) and (2), i.e. the linear TPF without and with dummies) conclusively show that if it is assumed that the TPF is linear (i.e. $f'=\beta$ and $f''=0$), all test results based on either of these equations give the same conclusions. And, these tests statistics show the linear TPF estimated from the full sample suffers from heteroscedasticity, but what is worse and more important, both equations (1) and (2) in Table 6.2(a) suffer from mis-specification problems. The RESET test statistics clearly show that, given the data, the linear TPF is not appropriate and this mis-specification in the TPF could be partly, if not totally, due to the assumption of linearity.

Here, the main objective of this is to test the linearity assumption explicitly and the author intends to use the Box-Cox specification of the TPF (equation (8)) for this purpose. Unfortunately, as (y-n) and (k-n) values for some countries are negative or zero and, as the Box-Cox model could not handle negative values (Bairam (1994)), in order to be able to use equation (8), the author could only use the 47 observations which have positive (y-n) and (k-n) rates, for estimation purposes.

Fortunately, the results obtained from the sub-sample of 47 observations for the Box-Cox production function estimates show that at least the static equations are not sensitive to sample changes. It can be seen that the production function parameters reported in Table 6.1(b) are very similar, or identical to, those parameters obtained from the full sample and are reported in Table 6.1(a).[42] The ϵ estimates (equation (6)) obtained using the parameter values from the sub-sample further proves this. It can be seen from the first two columns of the Appendix table that ϵ values obtained from the 47 observations for these countries are only around 0.03 lower than corresponding ϵ values obtained using the full sample results.

Given this assuring conclusion of non-sensitivity of the results to this sample change, equation (8) and its restricted version (i.e. $\lambda=1$, equation (4), the linear TPF) were estimated from the 47 observations. The results are reported in Table 6.2(b). First, it is clear that the two dummies included are not statistically significant so the discussion will focus on the two estimated equations without dummies − namely equations (1) and (2) in Table 2(b).[43]

---

[42] It is worthwhile to point out that since there are no oil exporting countries included in the sub-sample of 47 observations equation (5) estimates reported in Table 6.1(b) do not include O as dummy.

[43] However, once more, it is worthwhile to point out that if equations with the dummies were discussed, the conclusions would be the same.

Table 6.2(b)
The Linear and Non-Linear Technical Progress Function Sub-sample (n=47), Box-Cox Estimates
$$\{[(y-n)^{\lambda}-1]/\lambda\} = b_0 + b_2 D_2 + b_3 D_3 + \beta\{[(k-n)^{\lambda}-1]/\lambda\}$$

No.	b_1	b_2	b_3	β	λ	R^2	LLF	LRT
(1)	-0.963			0.46	0.47	0.471	158.55	
	(-7.64)			(6.47)				
(2)	0.012	-0.038	-0.006	0.43	1.00	0.462	153.99	10.88
	(5.57)	(-1.46)*	(-0.28)*	(6.37)				
(3)	-0.876			0.49	0.48	0.473	159.72	
	(-6.58)			(6.61)				
(4)	0.012	-0.006	-0.001	0.46	1.00	0.466	155.22	9.00
	(5.12)	(-1.49)*	(0.29)*	(6.52)				

Data Source: King and Levine (1994).
Notes: See text, Tables (6.1a), (6.1b) and (6.2a).

Turning first to finding the most appropriate specification of the TPF, the validity of the $\lambda=1$ restriction (i.e. linearity) was tested using the appropriate likelihood ratio test statistic. It is clear from this test statistic (12.62) that the linearity assumption is rejected. Therefore, given this data set, the technical progress function cannot be linear.

Turning next to explicitly testing the shape of the TPF, accepting the non-linear equation (1) in Table 6.2(b) as the correct specification, the f' and f" values for the 47 countries were computed using equations (9a) and (9b) in the text and the estimated equation in Table 6.2(b). These results are reported in the last two columns of the Appendix table. It can be seen from these values reported that f'>0 and f"<0 for all the countries under consideration.[44] Thus clearly confirming Kaldor's hypothesis that the technical progress "curve is likely to be convex upwards".

IV. CONCLUSION

In this paper the theory of technical progress functions were examined and its appropriate shape and underlying structure were tested.

It was shown that the linear TPF could be derived from the constant returns to scale Cobb-Douglas production function but test results showed that this is not the appropriate production function for the 107 countries under consideration. This could be interpreted as suggesting, if the TPF function has to be based on the appropriate underlying production function, it cannot be linear.

All the tests carried out on the linear TPF also clearly showed that the linear TPF is not appropriate for the countries under consideration. The appropriate function found out to be the one suggested by the economic theory and by Kaldor's original function (namely the one with f'>0 and f"<0)

Therefore, in summary, the main conclusion the author of this study has reached is that linearity is not supported by the data. However, this of course does not mean that a non-linear technical progress function cannot be derived from an appropriate non-linear (nonhomogeneous) production function. Indeed, most of the evidence presented here implies this is likely to be the case. However, this researcher believes before reaching a firm conclusion the appropriate underlying structure of the TPF should be further investigated.

---

[44] However, the f' and f" results also show that each country operates at different segments of the TPF and most developed OECD countries are operating at the flatter parts of the curve when compared with the less developed countries in the sample.

Appendix 6.1

Estimated ε, f' and f" Values by Country, the Sub-Sample Results, the 1980s

No.	Country Name	ε Results from: Full-	Sub-Sample	f' and f" results: from Sub-Sample	
1	Australia	0.62	0.57	0.51	-11.02
2	Austria	0.62	0.58	0.36	-2.55
3	Barbados	0.54	0.50	0.35	-2.87
4	Belgium	0.59	0.55	0.66	-26.02
5	Brazil	0.53	0.48	1.14	-336.29
6	Canada	0.57	0.53	0.37	-2.70
7	Columbia	0.50	0.45	0.48	-9.90
8	Congo	0.44	0.39	0.35	-1.52
9	Cyprus	0.61	0.58	0.66	-10.02
10	Denmark	0.62	0.59	1.02	-116.76
11	Egypt	0.34	0.29	0.32	-1.15
12	Finland	0.65	0.62	0.57	-9.04
13	France	0.61	0.57	0.45	-8.70
14	Germany	0.61	0.58	0.48	-8.76
15	Greece	0.59	0.55	0.50	-19.86
16	Hong Kong	0.49	0.45	0.47	-2.41
17	Iceland	0.58	0.53	0.52	-8.88
18	India	0.52	0.47	0.81	-25.51
19	Indonesia	0.53	0.48	0.29	-0.56
20	Ireland	0.63	0.60	0.56	-15.54
21	Israel	0.57	0.53	0.92	-87.88
22	Italy	0.60	0.56	0.47	-6.13
23	Japan	0.61	0.58	0.47	-4.11
24	Jordan	0.52	0.48	0.23	-0.33
25	Luxembourg	0.61	0.57	0.53	-7.41
26	Malaysia	0.60	0.56	0.34	-1.36
27	Mali	0.38	0.33	0.67	-51.27
28	Malta	0.56	0.52	0.36	-1.24
29	Mauritius	0.50	0.40	0.44	-3.22
30	Morocco	0.41	0.36	0.37	-3.15
31	Netherlands	0.58	0.54	0.73	-72.81
32	New Zealand	0.59	0.55	0.35	-4.49
33	Norway	0.64	0.61	0.50	-5.80
34	Panama	0.57	0.52	0.94	-69.68
35	Paraguay	0.45	0.40	0.21	-0.24
36	Portugal	0.57	0.53	0.51	-3.36
37	Singapore	0.59	0.55	0.38	-1.02
38	Spain	0.61	0.56	0.78	-38.22
39	Sri Lanka	0.57	0.53	0.40	-2.73
40	Sweden	0.58	0.54	0.56	-13.85
41	Switzerland	0.65	0.62	0.40	-4.10
42	Thailand	0.46	0.41	0.54	-5.24
43	Tunisia	0.46	0.42	0.86	-94.55
44	Turkey	0.55	0.51	0.43	-5.53
45	U.K.	0.54	0.50	0.47	-6.57
46	U.S.A.	0.53	0.48	0.39	-4.13
47	Uruguay	0.57	0.53	0.32	-26.33

Sources: Tables 6.1(a), 6.1(b), 6.2(b) and King and Levine (1994).
Notes: For the computation procedures and other notes, see text.

REFERENCES

Bairam, E.I. (1987), The Verdoorn law, returns to scale an industrial growth: a review of the literature, *Australian Economic Papers*, vol. 26, pp. 20-42.

Bairam, E.I. (1991), Elasticity of substitution, technical progress and returns to scale: a new CES production function approach, *Journal of Applied Econometrics*, vol. 6, pp. 91-96.

Bairam, E.I. (1994), *Homogeneous and Nonhomogeneous Production Functions: Theory and Applications*, Avebury, Aldershot

Black, J. (1962), The technical progress function and the production function, *Economica*, vol. 27, pp. 166-170.

Box, G.E.P. and Cox, D.R. (1964), An analysis of transformations, *Journal of Royal Statistical Society*, vol. 26 (series B), pp. 211-252.

Dixon, R. and Thirlwall, A.P. (1975), A model of regional growth differences on Kaldorian lines, *Oxford Economic Papers*, vol. 27, pp. 201-214.

Kaldor, N. (1957), A model for economic growth, *Economic Journal*, vol. 67, pp. 591-624.

King, R.G. and Levine, R. (1994), Capital fundamentalism, economic development and economic growth, *Carnegie-Rochester Conference Series on Public Policy*, Vol. 40.

White, K.J. (1978), A general computer program for econometric methods-shazam, *Econometrica*, vol. 46. pp. 239-40.

7 The Measurement of Technical Change and the Estimation of Factor Demand

Chris Doucouliagos and
Phillip Hone[45]

I. INTRODUCTION

The impact of technical change on factor demand and on production costs is important for policy makers concerned with employment and structural change. Thus, it is important that technical change be included in the specification of a production system and it is also important that technical change be measured properly. Mispecification and measurement errors may lead to biased parameter estimates and limit the use of empirical analysis to policy makers. The purpose of this paper is to explore the impact of three alternative measures of technical change on the estimated elasticities derived from cost functions.

This exploration is undertaken by estimating variable cost functions for the Australian dairy processing industry, using time series data for the period 1969 to 1994. The diary processing industry is an interesting case because despite growth in product demand, employment has fallen substantially in this industry, across all producing states. For example, over the 1969 to 1994 period, employment in Victoria (the key producer state) fell at an average annual rate of about 1 percent. The industry as a whole experienced a decline in employment of about 1.7 percent per annum, on average. Thus, it seems appropriate to investigate the movements in the demand for factors of production in this industry, and the extent to which technical change has been an important contributor.

The results suggest that the estimated elasticities are sensitive to the measure of technical change used. This indicates that caution should be

---

[45] An earlier version of this paper was presented at the Econometrics Society Australasian meeting 1997, where helpful comments were received from Harry Bloch, Tim Coelli and other participants. The research was supported by a grant from the Faculty of Business and Law, Deakin University.

exercised when assessing the impact of technical change on factor demand and interpreting the results of many of the existing studies.

The specification and measurement issues are discussed in section II. The impact of alternative measures of technical change is explored in section III. Some directions for future research are noted in section IV.

II. THE MEASUREMENT OF TECHNICAL CHANGE

The measure of technical change should reflect: "the output change not accounted for by changes in inputs and the input mix" (Morrison, 1993, p. 45). The impact of technical change is normally incorporated into a cost function by using a linear time trend. The use of a linear time trend assumes that technical change can be summarised by some constant relationship and that it is always proceeding. However, technical change does not proceed at a constant pace and it can halt or decline over certain periods. Thus, it is highly unlikely that a linear time trend will represent adequately the underlying technical change process (see Diewert and Wales (1992) and Fox (1998)).[46] This would not be such a problem if the extent and direction of the bias in estimated elasticities when using a time trend, was known. Unfortunately, it may be the case that the bias in the elasticity estimates derived from functions where a linear time trend represents technical change, cannot be determined *a priori*.

A promising line of research involves the use of spline functions (piecewise polynomials), where a more flexible representation of the time trend is introduced (see Fox, 1998). While this approach has much intellectual merit, in this paper we adopt an alternative approach, by using a measure of total factor productivity. The use of splines represents substantial progress in the measurement of technical change. Splines allow the rate of technical progress to vary over the sample and over sub-periods. An encouraging way of doing this has been proposed by Fox (1998). However, in order to identify the appropriate spline function, analysts may have to compare the fitted spline against a raw measure of total factor productivity. That is, the specification of a spline function is not necessarily independent of the total factor productivity measure.

Conceptually, the use of a total factor productivity measure is preferable to using a linear time trend. The use of a measure of total factor productivity as a proxy for technical change has two benefits. First, it is derived directly from production and cost data and is thus derived with reference to this data. Second, since total factor

---

[46] Watts and Quiggin (1984) note that it is also not appropriate to use a logarithmic time trend, as this leads to biased results.

productivity movements are not linear, they represent a more flexible and more accurate representation of technical change, allowing for varying rates of technical progress, technical stagnation and even technical regression.[47]

The use of total factor productivity is not necessarily the best way of measuring technical change (some suggestions for improved measures are offered in section III). We concur with many of the criticisms made against total factor productivity measures. For example, Morrison (1993, p. 34) notes that: "Measured productivity could, for example, include changes in scale economies or capacity utilization as well as technical change."

Morrison has argued (1993, p. 59) that traditional measures of capacity utilisation are inappropriate as they are: "not based on analysis of the production structure in general, the numbers are difficult to interpret because the peaks are not equal and there is no explanation of why they differ, yet all are called "1.00"."

Morrison (1993) is correct to argue that the proper way to adjust measures of total factor productivity for variations in scale and capacity utilisation is to estimate a structural variable cost function.[48] Morrison recommends a two step procedure. The first step involves the estimation of a variable cost function using a linear time trend as a proxy for technical change. The second step is to use the parameter estimates to adjust the raw total factor productivity measure for variations in scale and capacity utilisation.[49]

Using similar procedures, Berndt and Fuss (1986), Berndt and Hesse (1986), Hulten (1986) and Morrison (1986 and 1989) corrected total factor productivity measures for capacity utilisation and found the differences from doing so to be small in general, although the differences were important for some years. The impact of these adjustments, is as noted by Morrison "a slight smoothing of the numbers" (1993, p. 205). Nevertheless, since the corrected measures are likely to be closer to the real picture, they are more accurate and should be used. More substantial differences were uncovered by Morrison (1989), where the correction for scale and capacity utilisation was very important.

---

[47] While technical regression is not a normal expectation, conceptually it is preferable that the measure of technical change be flexible enough to allow for it.

[48] As noted by Morrison (1993) and Berndt and Fuss (1989), the use of a structural model to estimate capacity utilisation, when there are several fixed inputs, becomes very difficult.

[49] The full procedure for making the relevant adjustments is discussed in Morrison (1993).

In this paper, total factor productivity was adjusted for capacity utilisation using the 'peak-to-peak' method.[50] While this is not the ideal procedure, it does go part of the way of identifying the path of technical progress. The cost based capacity utilisation adjustments require that the cost function be well behaved with respect to the shadow price of capital, which in many cases it was not. Further, the two step procedure itself may be prone to error at the first stage because of the use of a time counter. Since the interest here is on the impact of different measures of technical change on factor demand and given that the appropriate strategy is not clear, we retain the traditional 'peak-to-peak' procedure of adjusting for capacity utilisation.

A second problem with the use of the total factor productivity measure is that it is a generated regressor. Pagan (1984) has shown that it is important that generated regressors be interpreted cautiously. The generation of the total factor productivity measure is subject to some error. This means that the standard errors for the terms associated with technical change will be biased downward. Ideally, this error should be taken into account in the estimation of the cost function and share equation. The total factor productivity measure was derived from a non-parametric procedure so that the derivation of the variance is not straightforward. It is not obvious how the standard errors should be corrected for the generated regressor problem in this framework.[51] Quandt and Rosen (1988) have argued that biased standard errors can result from several other causes and that in many cases it is not possible to correct for the generated regressor problem. They conclude that: "Applied econometricians should always present their results with some humility" (1988, p. 75).

It should be noted that the impact of changes in total factor productivity on both costs and factor demand may be of interest in its own right. Researchers may very well be interested in the impact of a capacity unadjusted or gross measure of total factor productivity on costs. For example, if output does fall by a greater percentage than inputs because of input hoarding, then the impact of hoarding on costs may be captured by using the gross measure.

i) **Measuring total factor productivity**

Total factor productivity is usually measured either by the Törnqvist procedure or by the Fisher Ideal Price Index. Both the Törnqvist and the Fisher Ideal index procedures are superlative. That is, they are exact for the underlying production functions which they represent. The Törnqvist index represents a translog production function and the

---

[50] The capacity utilisation series for the Australian dairy industry varies to a greater extent than does the associated capacity utlisation series for GDP for Australia, as a whole.

[51] For example, the techniques used by Gawande (1997) cannot be used here.

Fisher Ideal index represents a quadratic production function. However, it is well known that the Törnqvist procedure does not pass the factor reversal tests (see Diewert 1992 and 1993a). Thus, our preferred measure was the Fisher ideal index which does pass the factor reversal test, as well as several other statistical tests which an index procedure should have (see Diewert 1992 and 1993a). The Fisher ideal index is measured as the geometric mean of the Laspeyres and Paasche indices.

Two such indices were constructed. The preferred measure was constructed using real turnover as the measure of output and labour, capital stock and milk as the three inputs. This measure of total factor productivity is consistent with the construction of a two variable and one fixed input cost function. The second measure of total factor productivity was based on a value added specification. In this formulation, output was proxied by value added, with labour as the one variable input and capital stock as the one fixed input.

The idea behind constructing this measure is to test the impact of a different specification of total factor productivity on parameter and elasticity estimates. Researchers may not have the choice of which measure to use. For example, researchers may have data on labour and capital stock inputs but no data on raw materials. This means that they can only construct a value added specification of total factor productivity. However, in the context of a three input production process, it is clear that the turnover specification is preferable. The actual total factor productivity series for Australia and for each state can be found in Doucouliagos and Hone (1997).

ii) The variable translog cost function

There are several empirical flexible cost functions which place no *a priori* restrictions on the Allen partial elasticities of substitution. In this paper the parameter estimates are derived from a translog variable cost function. Many authors continue to use a translog total cost function. For example, in one of the relatively few studies of interrelated factor demand using Australian manufacturing data, Truett and Truett (1996) estimated an interrelated translog total cost function. However, it is reasonable to assume that capital is a fixed input rather than assuming that capital stock can be adjusted readily in response to exogenous input price changes. The assumption of capital as a fixed input makes particularly good sense when time series data are used.

In its general form the translog variable cost function is given by:

$$\ln VC = \alpha_0 + \beta_Y \ln Y + \beta_L \ln P_L + \beta_M \ln P_M + \beta_K \ln K$$
$$+ \beta_T T + \frac{1}{2} \beta_{TT} (T)^2 + \frac{1}{2} \beta_{YY} (\ln Y)^2$$
$$+ \frac{1}{2} \beta_{LL} (\ln P_L)^2 + \frac{1}{2} \beta_{MM} (\ln P_M)^2 + \frac{1}{2} \beta_{KK} (\ln K)^2$$
$$+ \beta_{LM} \ln P_L \ln P_M + \beta_{YL} \ln Y \ln P_L + \beta_{YM} \ln Y \ln P_M$$

$$+ \beta_{YK}\ln Y \ln K + \beta_{KL}\ln K \ln P_L + \beta_{KM}\ln K \ln P_M + \beta_{TL}\ln T \ln P_L$$
$$+ \beta_{TM}\ln T \ln P_M + \beta_{TY}\ln T \ln Y + \beta_{TK}\ln T \ln K \qquad (1)$$

where VC are variable costs (the wage bill plus the value of milk purchased), Y is real output measured by real turnover, P_L is the unit price of labour, P_M is the unit price of milk, K is the real capital stock and T is a measure of technical change.

The general nature of this functional form is illustrated in Figure 7.1. Total variable cost is a positive function of both the level of output and the price of the variable input, which in the case of Figure 7.1 is labour. Changes in the level of the fixed input, capital, vertically displace the cost surface oedc. For example, if the shadow value of capital exceeds the market price of capital, then as the level of capital increases, the cost surface pivots on the labour price axis to yield lower levels of variable costs for all positive, non-zero levels of output.

In terms of the cost surface in Figure 7.1, the impact of technological change is equivalent to downwards displacement in cost surface oedc. Depending on the nature of the technological change, the general shape of the cost surface could also change.

Four assumptions are necessary in order to estimate this translog variable cost function. First, we assume that labour and milk prices are exogenous to the firm. Second, the firm is free to vary the quantity of labour and milk used, but in the short run faces a fixed capital stock. Third, it is assumed that errors are random and reflect random deviations from optimality. Thus, in common with other researchers in this area we ignore the important issue of technical and allocative efficiency, and assume that firms are all economically efficient.

In addition to the variable cost function itself, Shephard's lemma is used to derive input cost shares, representing cost minimising factor demands:

$$\frac{\partial \ln VC}{\partial \ln P_L} = \frac{P_L L}{VC} = \beta_L + \beta_{LL}\ln P_L + \beta_{LM}\ln P_M + \beta_{KL}\ln K$$
$$+ \beta_{YL}\ln Y + \beta_{TL}\ln T$$

$$\frac{\partial \ln VC}{\partial \ln P_M} = \frac{P_M M}{VC} = \beta_M + \beta_{LM}\ln P_L + \beta_{MM}\ln P_M + \beta_{KM}\ln K$$
$$+ \beta_{YM}\ln Y + \beta_{TM}\ln T \qquad (2)$$

The variable labour cost share plus the variable milk cost share sum to one, so that it is necessary to estimate only one of the cost share equations. The variable cost function should be homogeneous of

Table 7.1

Sequential Tests for Homotheticity and Homogeneity
(Turnover based measure of total factor productivity)

	Homotheticity		Homogeneity	
	adjusted for capacity utilisation	*not adjusted for capacity utilisation*	*adjusted for capacity utilisation*	*not adjusted for capacity utilisation*
NSW	reject (p=0.00)	accept (p=0.14)	na	reject (p=0.06)
VIC	reject (p=0.00)	reject (p=0.06)	na	na
QLD	reject (p=0.00)	accept (p=0.61)	na	accept (p=0.81)
SA	reject (p=0.00)	reject (p=0.00)	na	na
TAS	accept (p=0.50)	accept (p=0.60)	reject (p=0.00)	reject (p=0.00)
WA	reject (p=0.00)	reject (p=0.00)	na	na
Australia	reject (p=0.00)	reject (p=0.00)	na	na

degree 1 in variable input prices. Imposing this condition and deleting the milk cost share equation yields the following cost share equation:[52]

$$S_{VCL} = \beta_L + \beta_{LL} \ln(P_L/P_M) + \beta_{KL} \ln K + \beta_{YL} \ln Y + \beta_{TL} \ln T \quad (3)$$

Equation 3 is estimated jointly with the variable cost function.[53] The coefficients for the milk variable cost share can be recovered from the estimated parameters. The elasticities of substitution and the price elasticities can be calculated from the fitted cost shares and from the estimated parameters.

The translog variable cost function was estimated for each state, as the separate state estimates may pick up important differences in substitution possibilities. Moreover, since the Australian wide data are aggregates of the state data, a comparison of state and total estimates can shed light on the extent of any aggregation bias. This is important, as most of the existing literature focuses on aggregate manufacturing data, even though the real story lies in as much disaggregation as possible.[54] Also, the data from the different states provides an enlarged data set from which to test for differences in the measurement of technical change. A full description of the data set can be found in Doucouliagos and Hone (1997), with a brief description offered in Appendix.

The two variable and one fixed input model is obviously limited. We have not considered the input of energy. The omission of an important variable, such as energy or raw materials, is usually justified through the Leontief aggregation condition, or the Hicksian aggregation condition, or by the separability condition (see Berndt and Wood, 1975).[55] We do not believe that these conditions hold for our data set. This suggests that the results presented in the paper may be biased. Note, however, that there are many inputs into the production process and omitting them can lead to misspecification problems. This problem is common to most empirical studies of factor demand. For

---

[52] The price of milk has been used as the normalising variable, in order to avoid singularity in the disturbance covariance and residual cross-products matrices. Since the estimation technique used is Iterative Seemingly Unrelated Regression, then the choice of the normalising variable is irrelevant.

[53] Econometric Views Version 2 was used to derive all the estimates.

[54] However, it is clear that the state data are aggregates of firm level data, where the real story lies.

[55] In the context of the results presented in this paper, the Leontief aggregation condition holds if the elasticity of substitution between energy and all other inputs is constant and is equal to zero, or $\sigma_{EE} = \sigma_{EM} = \sigma_{LE} = \sigma_{KE} = 0$, where E denotes energy inputs. The Hicksian aggregation condition holds if the price of energy and the price of output move together. The separability condition holds if the capital, labour and raw material inputs are weakly separable from energy.

example, managerial input is surely vital to the production process but how often is it incorporated into the estimation process? In this case we are confident that we are capturing the contributions of the key inputs; the milk, labour and capital inputs are the major inputs into the dairy processing industry.

Six important limitations with this paper should be noted. First, we do not incorporate expectations into the modelling strategy and estimation procedure. Second, it is well known that the translog cost function (total or variable) and the production function are not self-dual (see, for example, Applebaum (1978) and Burgess (1975)). This means that the elasticities of substitution and associated price elasticities may differ depending on whether the production or cost functions are estimated. We do not compare our results with those derived from a production function. Third, it is possible that the results from the variable cost function may differ to those derived from the profit function. Fourth, we do not consider dynamics. Hence, we do not offer estimates of adjustment speeds nor do we provide any information on whether factor demand may be affected by slow response in adjusting other inputs. Fifth, we do not compare the results for each State to those derived from pooling the data. Analysis of time series data provides some insights into the short run elasticities and adjustment process, while analysis of the pooled data is more likely to offer information on the long run (see Griffin and Gregory, 1976). Finally, there has been much (some would say an excessive) attention to the degree of integration of a time series and to the dangers of spurious regression (see Charemza and Deadman, 1992). Most researchers of interrelated factor demand have ignored these concerns (see, for example, the review by Hamermesh (1993)). This is particularly important, as the traditional way of correcting for the existence of trends in time series data was to include a time trend. However, in keeping with standard practice in the literature and in order to facilitate comparisons with other studies (see Morrison, 1993) in this paper we do not apply a first difference filter.[56] These six complicating issues can be abstracted from safely, since the aim of this paper is to explore the impact of the differences in the measurement of technical change.

III. PARAMETER ESTIMATES FROM TRANSLOG VARIABLE COST FUNCTIONS

The translog variable cost function set out in equations 1 and 2 above is a general heterothetic function. Rather than imposing homotheticity or homogeneity, it is now standard practice to test for the validity of these

---

[56] When the first difference filter is applied, even greater differences in the estimated elasticities emerge. These results are available from the authors.

restrictions. It is interesting to explore whether differences in the measurement of technical change lead to differences in the test results. It is also of interest to explore what impact the adjustment for variation in capacity utilisation has on the test results. The tests where conducted sequentially. That is, if the homotheticity restriction was supported then this was imposed and the homogeneity restriction was then tested. The results from this testing procedure using the turnover based measure, the value added based measure and the linear time trend are listed in Tables 7.1, 7.2 and 7.3, respectively.[57]

A comparison of Tables 7.1, 7.2 and 7.3 shows that the way technical change is measured, and the use of data not adjusted for capacity utilisation do make a difference to the test results in several cases.

The parameters from the estimated variable cost function applied to the Australian data are listed in Table 7.4, using total factor productivity indices adjusted for capacity utilisation. The adjusted R-squared for the total cost function is denoted by $\overline{R}_c^2$ and the adjusted R-squared for the labour cost share equation is denoted by $\overline{R}_L^2$. The Durbin-Watson statistic for the cost share equation is DW_c and for the labour cost share equation it is DW_L. It is well known that the conventional single equation goodness of fit measures are not adequate for a system of equations. We thus also provide the Wald test statistic (testing whether all the slope coefficients in all equations are simultaneously equal to zero).

All the goodness of fit measures are reasonable. In all cases the Durbin-Watson statistic provides inconclusive evidence of the presence or absence of autocorrelation. While the equations could be reestimated and corrected for autocorrelation (if it exists), the autocorrelation probably reflects misspecification. A dynamic respecification of the cost function should overcome this autocorrelation.[58]

The elasticities of substitution and price elasticities are presented in Tables 7.5, 7.6 and 7.7, for the estimates derived when using the turnover based measure of total factor productivity, a linear time trend, and the value added based measure of total factor productivity,

---

[57] For tables 7.1, 7.2 and 7.3, the global test for homotheticity is $\beta_{TL}=\beta_{TK}=\beta_{TY}=0$. The sequential test for homogeneity is $\beta_{TY}=0$, conducted after the homotheticity restriction was imposed (in those cases where this restriction was accepted). The Chi square test statistics are not listed but are available from the authors.

[58] Because the issue of dynamics has been ignored, we have not tested for the existence of common factors. The static models with autocorrelation may be acceptable substitutes to the general model.

respectively.[59] Figures in bold are those with an unexpected or incorrect sign. The symbols used are listed below:

ε_{LL} the own price elasticity of labour
ε_{MM} the own price elasticity of milk
σ_{ML} the elasticity of substitution between milk and labour
ε_{CY} the elasticity of variable costs with respect to output
ε_{CT} the elasticity of variable costs with respect to technical change
ε_{LT} the elasticity of labour with respect to technical change
ε_{MT} the elasticity of milk with respect to technical change

For this data set, the use of the linear time trend led, in many cases, to either incorrectly signed elasticities or unexpected elasticities. For example, a negative ε_{CY} (estimated for Western Australia, South Australia and Tasmania) is clearly not correct.[60] The signs on the elasticities with respect to technical change are also of some concern. A conclusion drawn from Table 7.6 is that for two of the states, technical change has no impact on variable costs and in the case of Queensland it actually increases costs. While these results are theoretically possible, industry knowledge suggests that these are incorrect. For example, it is not likely that technical change has had no impact at all on variable costs in Victoria. Victoria is the key producing state and Victorian firms have placed much effort on technical change; they would not have done so if there were no cost savings flowing from this.

In all cases, the linear time trend results in smaller technical change elasticities than the turnover based measure of total factor productivity. This suggests that the *direction* of this bias may be predictable. For this data set at least, the time trend in general understates these elasticities. There is no obvious pattern with respect to the other elasticities, which may be understated or overstated, although the magnitude of the differences are generally small.

From a policy point of view an important issue is often whether the elasticities are elastic or inelastic. This issue does not emerge for this data set. For example, for Queensland the own price elasticity for labour when the linear time trend is used is -0.18, but is -0.33 when the turnover total factor productivity measure is used. Such differences are not very important. However, there is a significant difference in economic terms in the elasticity of milk intake with respect to technical change; which for Queensland is +0.02 when the time trend is used and -0.54 when turnover total factor productivity is used. It does make a

---

[59] All the elasticities in tables 7.5, 7.6 and 7.7 were evaluated at the mean of the *fitted* cost shares.
[60] The negative sign on the elasticity of substitution between milk and labour, recorded for Australia when the turnover based measure of technical change was used is also incorrect. This result can be attributed to aggregation problems.

qualitative difference to policy when one measure of technical change suggests a milk using response of factor demand to technical change and another measure of technical change suggests a milk saving response.

The bias in technical change is also important to policy makers. This is reflected in the difference between the ε_{LT} and ε_{MT} coefficients. Using the results from Table 7.5, it can be concluded that technical change is both labour saving and milk saving but it is effectively biased in favour of milk. That is, the savings are greater for labour in all states and for Australia as a whole, except in the case of Queensland and Tasmania, where a milk saving bias emerges. A similar conclusion can be drawn, generally, when the time trend is used (see Table 7.6), except that the bias in technical change is much smaller.

It was disappointing that the variable cost function was not well behaved. While the first order condition was met for each state, the second order conditions were generally not.[61] There are at least five possibilities for this. First, the data may not be of a sufficient quality to estimate a well behaved cost function. Given that the analysis from the aggregate Australia wide data led to different results, we are led to believe that the state data may also suffer from aggregation bias (over numerous plants). This makes it desirable that plant level data be used to test theoretical cost predictions. Second, the translog function may not be an adequate representation of the underlying cost conditions. Thus, comparison of these results with alternative general cost functions seems appropriate.[62] Third, neoclassical cost functions may not be an accurate representation of a firm's behaviour. Fourth, we have not considered expectations in the estimation procedure and we have not considered adjustment costs. Both of these are clearly important. The incorporation of dynamics and expectations should yield a closer approximation to the underlying cost conditions. Finally, it may be the case that over the period investigated, it is possible that firms were in disequilibrium and for some of this period could have been making sub-optimal decisions. Since our estimation procedure did not allow for this, then it is not surprising that the cost curves did not satisfy second order conditions.

The results presented here on the sensitivity of elasticities to the specification of technical change are discouraging. One of the common reasons for using a translog cost function is that the data necessary to estimate a production function is lacking. For example, a researcher may have input prices but no measure of capital stock or labour input.

---

[61] The cost function is well behaved if it is strictly quasi-concave in input prices and if the σ_{ij} matrix is negative semidefinite. This latter condition was not satisfied for several years.

[62] We are reluctant, however, to use functions which impose expected conditions. Such an approach does not test theory.

If this is so, then the data to estimate a total factor productivity measure is also lacking. If it is not possible to predict *a priori* the impact on the estimated elasticities, associated with the use of a time trend, then researchers without all the relevant production data face a major problem. If a time trend is not included, then the estimated model is constructed on the assumption that technical change has no impact on factor demand. This is clearly unrealistic. However, if the time trend is included, then the results may be biased by an unknown degree and direction. Several authors who have included a time trend found that the functions did not perform well (see for example Truett and Truett, 1996), as was also the case in Table 7.6. Moreover, if the time trend is found to be insignificant, this does not necessarily mean that technical change is insignificant, rather it may mean that technical change does not proceed at a constant pace.

IV. SUGGESTIONS FOR FUTURE RESEARCH

Industry knowledge tells us that technical change should be included in a variable cost function. The issue however is how technical change should be measured. Care should be exercised in the representation of technical change and its impact on factor demand. There are problems with both the use of a time trend as well as with the total factor productivity measures of technical change.

There are at least two different ways to proceed from here. First, it is important to devise a strategy for correcting the measures of total factor productivity for variations in capacity utilisation. Second, it is also important to separate changes in technical and allocative efficiency from total factor productivity. That is, to separate shifts in the production frontier from movements towards the frontier.

Perhaps some sort of iterative estimation procedure is necessary to achieve the first task. For example, it may be appropriate to modify the procedure outlined by Morrison (1993). The first step could be the use of a raw total factor productivity measure in the variable cost function. The parameter estimates from this first step could then be used to adjust the total factor productivity index for variations in capacity utilisation. The third step could then be to reestimate the variable cost function using the adjusted total factor productivity series.

The second task may be achieved by using frontier estimation techniques. These techniques could be used to derive a measure of the extent of scale, technical and allocative inefficiency among decision making units, as well as measuring total factor productivity. The derived total factor productivity measure would then be net of changes in technical and allocative inefficiency. This measure of total factor productivity could then be used in the estimation of a cost function. It may also be possible to integrate these two procedures. If procedures such as these generate more reliable measures of technical change, then they should lead to improved estimates of the impact of technical change on factor demand.

Table 7.2

Sequential Tests for Homotheticity and Homogeneity,
(Value added based measure of total factor productivity)

	Homotheticity		Homogeneity	
	adjusted for capacity utilisation	*not adjusted for capacity utilisation*	*adjusted for capacity utilisation*	*not adjusted for capacity utilisation*
NSW	reject (p=0.00)	accept (p=0.96)	na	accept (p=0.36)
VIC	reject (p=0.00)	accept (p=0.94)	na	accept (p=0.85)
QLD	reject (p=0.02)	reject (p=0.01)	na	na
SA	reject (p=0.02)	accept (p=0.11)	na	accept (p=0.90)
TAS	accept (p=0.22)	accept (p=0.12)	accept (p=0.35)	accept (p=0.31)
WA	reject (p=0.00)	reject (p=0.00)	na	na
Australia	reject (p=0.04)	accept (p=0.15)	na	accept (p=0.50)

Table 7.3

Sequential Tests for Homotheticity and Homogeneity, (Time trend measure of technical change)

	homotheticity	homogeneity
NSW	reject (p=0.01)	na
VIC	reject (p=0.00)	na
QLD	accept (p=0.58)	reject (p=0.05)
SA	reject (p=0.00)	na
TAS	reject (p=0.00)	na
WA	accept (p=0.39)	reject (p=0.02)
Australia	reject (p=0.02)	na

Table 7.4

Translog Variable Cost Function Parameter Estimates for Australian Dairy Products Manufacturing 1969-1994 (t statistics)

	Turnover TFP	Value Added TFP	Time Trend
α_0	50.12 (12.06)***	-14.42 (-0.18)	-8.88 (0.25)
β_L	2.07 (11.90)***	0.87 (3.63)***	1.18 (3.70)***
β_{LL}	0.21 (23.23)***	0.18 (13.66)***	0.19 (16.45)***
β_K	-17.51 (-3.60)***	50.05 (1.07)	23.39 (0.99)
β_{KK}	3.12 (2.07)**	-9.33 (-1.05)	-18.76 (-2.53)**
β_{LK}	-0.20 (-2.24)**	0.13 (1.60)	0.05 (0.51)
β_Y	-8.23 (-4.41)***	-17.19 (-0.83)	-15.37 (-1.77)*
β_{YY}	0.54 (0.43)	10.57 (1.92)*	0.35 (0.15)
β_T	-3.50 (-4.03)***	-6.74 (-0.94)	0.10 (0.49)
β_{TT}	0.64 (7.33)***	0.25 (0.70)	0.004 (5.63)***
β_{LT}	-0.005 (-0.27)	-0.06 (-5.33)***	-0.003 (-2.87)**
β_{KT}	0.65 (1.95)**	3.11 (1.62)	0.005 (0.08)
β_{YT}	0.21 (0.95)	-0.42 (-0.33)	-0.05 (-1.51)
β_{YL}	-0.23 (-3.65)***	-0.12 (-2.47)**	-0.16 (-2.62)**
β_{YK}	2.34 (1.59)	-8.64 (-0.87)	6.08 (1.75)*
Wald test	76,564,566 (p=0.00)	4,579,583 (p=0.00)	530,927.3 (p=0.00)
$\overline{R}_c^2$	0.99	0.99	0.99
$\overline{R}_L^2$	0.73	0.87	0.79
DW_C	0.67	0.64	0.92
DW_L	0.79	0.73	0.74

*,**,*** statistically significant at the 10%, 5% and 1% levels, respectively.

Table 7.5

Elasticities from Translog Variable Cost Functions, using turnover tfp
(Adjusted for capacity utilisation)

	Australia	VIC	NSW	QLD	WA	SA	TAS
ε_{LL}	0.02	-0.19	-0.16	-0.33	-0.11	-0.20	-0.14
ε_{MM}	0.01	-0.04	-0.05	-0.08	-0.04	-0.05	-0.03
σ_{ML}	-0.03	0.23	0.22	0.41	0.15	0.25	0.16
ε_{CY}	0.35	1.00	0.06	0.23	0.59	0.59	0.40
ε_{CT}	-0.31	-0.11	-0.18	-0.43	-0.23	-0.13	-0.29
ε_{LT}	-0.37	-0.33	-0.31	-0.21	-0.37	-0.37	-0.27
ε_{MT}	-0.34	-0.08	-0.16	-0.54	-0.22	-0.09	-0.33

Table 7.6

Elasticities from Translog Variable Cost Functions, using linear time trend

	Australia	VIC	NSW	QLD	WA	SA	TAS
ε_{LL}	-0.03	0.05	-0.01	-0.18	-0.29	-0.23	-0.86
ε_{MM}	-0.01	0.01	-0.004	-0.04	-0.09	-0.06	-0.35
σ_{ML}	0.03	-0.06	0.01	0.23	0.38	0.29	1.21
ε_{CY}	0.62	0.21	0.13	0.28	-0.16	-0.31	-0.20
ε_{CT}	-0.01	0.00	-0.02	0.02	0.00	-0.02	-0.08
ε_{LT}	-0.02	-0.02	-0.03	0.00	-0.01	-0.05	-0.08
ε_{MT}	-0.01	0.00	-0.01	0.02	0.01	-0.01	-0.10

Table 7.7

Elasticities from Translog Variable Cost Functions, using value tfp
(Adjusted for capacity utilisation)

	Australia	VIC	NSW	QLD	WA	SA	TAS
ε_{LL}	-0.10	-0.34	0.08	-0.14	-0.21	-0.36	-0.21
ε_{MM}	-0.02	-0.08	0.03	-0.03	-0.07	-0.09	-0.03
σ_{ML}	0.12	0.42	-0.11	0.18	0.28	0.45	0.24
ε_{CY}	0.44	0.18	0.24	0.67	0.26	0.54	1.08
ε_{CT}	-3.23	-0.10	-0.20	-0.12	-0.12	-0.08	-0.66
ε_{LT}	-2.02	-0.28	-0.44	-0.19	-0.28	-0.25	-0.75
ε_{MT}	-1.67	-0.08	-0.16	-0.12	-0.10	-0.04	-0.73

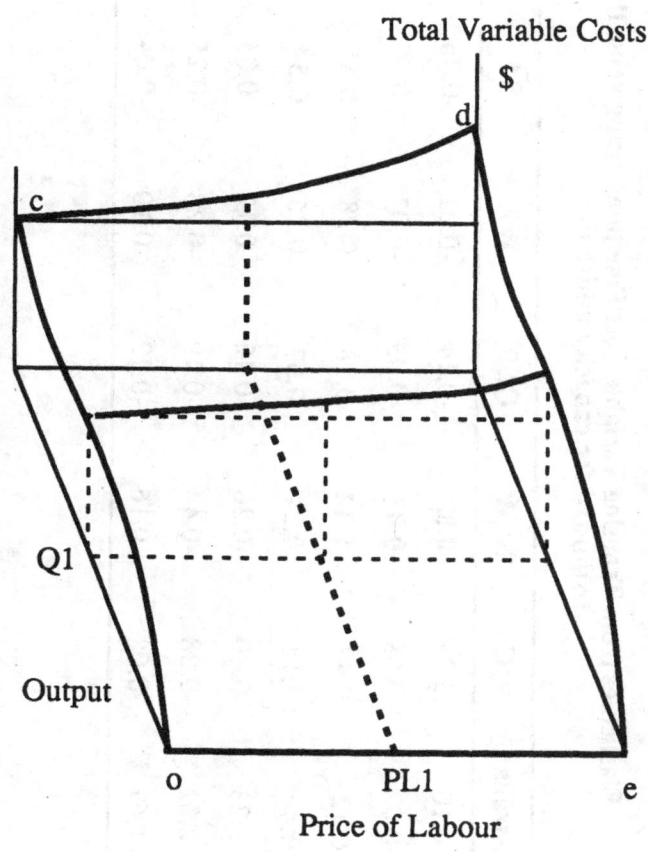

Figure 7.1 The Variable Cost Surface

Appendix - Data sources and transformations

A full discussion of the data collection and construction structure can be found in Doucouliagos and Hone (1997).

Output: Real value added was estimated as the value of the industry's turnover plus change in stocks less purchases deflated by a price index of articles produced by the dairy processing industries.

Labour Input: Aggregate hours worked was estimated by adjusting the number of workers employed in each year and in each State by the average number of hours worked in the dairy processing industry in each State.

Milk Intake: Data on the volume and gross value of milk production was derived from Australian Bureau of Agricultural and Resource Economics, *Commodity Statistical Bulletin*, various issues.

Capital Stock: The perpetual inventory method was used to estimate capital stock. Separate capital stock estimates were derived for plant and equipment and for buildings, using a series on net (after disposals) capital expenditure. Data limitations prevented the inclusion of rent and leasing of equipment.

REFERENCES

Applebaum, E. (1978), Testing Neoclassical Production Theory, *Journal of Econometrics*, Vol. 7, No. 1, pp. 87-102.

Berndt, Ernst R. and Fuss, Melvyn (1986), Productivity Measurement With Adjustments for Capacity Utilisation and other forms of Temporary Equilibrium, *Journal of Econometrics*, Vol. 33, No. 1/2 (October/November), pp. 7-29.

Berndt, Ernst R. and Fuss, Melvyn (1989), Economic Capacity Utilization and Productivity Measurement for Multiproduct Firms with Multiple Quasi-Fixed Inputs, *National Bureau of Economic Research Working Paper*, No. 2932, April.

Berndt, E.R. and Hesse, Dieter M. (1986), Measuring and Assessing Capacity Utilization in the Manufacturing Sectors of Nine OECD Countries, *European Economic Review*, Vol. 30, No. 5 (October), pp. 961-989.

Berndt, Ernst R. and Wood, David O. (1975), Technology, Prices and the Derived Demand for Energy, *Review of Economics and Statistics*, Vol. 57, No. 3 (August), pp. 259-268.

Berndt, Ernst R. and Wood, David O. (1982), The Specification and Measurement of Technical Change in U.S. Manufacturing, chapter 7,

John R. Moroney ed., *Advances in the Economics of Energy and Natural Resources*, Vol. 4, pp. 199-221, JAI Press, Greenwich, Conn.

Bureau of Industry Economics (1985), *Productivity Growth in Australian Manufacturing Industry: 1954-55 to 1981-82*, Information Bulletin No. 8, Australian Government Publishing Service, Canberra.

Burgess, D.F. (1975), Duality Theory and Pitfalls in the Specification of Technologies, *Journal of Econometrics*, Vol. 3, No. 2, pp. 105-121.

Charemza, Wojciech W. and Deadman, Derek F. (1992), *New Directions in Econometric Practice*, Edward Elgar, Aldershot.

Diewert, W.E. (1976), Exact and Superlative Index Numbers, *Journal of Econometrics*, Vol. 4, pp. 115-145.

Diewert, W.E. (1978), Superlative Index Numbers and Consistency in Aggregation, *Econometrica*, Vol. 46, pp. 883-900.

Diewert, W.E. (1992), Fisher Ideal Output, Input and Productivity Indexes Revisited, *Journal of Productivity Analysis*, Vol. 3, pp. 211-248.

Diewert, W.E. (1993a), The Measurement of Productivity: A Survey, paper presented to *Measuring the Economic Performance of Government Enterprises*, Swan Consultants (Canberra) Pty Ltd Conference.

Diewert, W.E. (1993b), International Benchmarking - What is Best Practice?, paper presented to *Measuring the Economic Performance of Government Enterprises*, Swan Consultants (Canberra) Pty Ltd Conference.

Diewert, W.E. and Wales, T.J. (1992), Quadratic Spline Models for Producer's Supply and Demand Functions, *International Economic Review*, Vol. 33, pp. 705-722.

Doucouliagos, Chris and Hone, Phillip (1997), Total Factor Productivity In Australian Dairy Manufacturing, School of Economics, Faculty of Business and Law, Deakin University, Working Paper, No. 22.

Fox, Kevin J. (1998), Non-Parametric Estimation of Technical Progress, *Journal of Productivity Analysis*, Vol. 10, No. 3, forthcoming.

Garofalo, Gaspar and Malhotra, Devinder (1984), Input Substitution in the Manufacturing Sector during the 1970s: A Regional Analysis, *Journal of Regional Science*, Vol. 24, pp. 51-63.

Gawande, Kishore (1997), Generated Regressors in Linear and Nonlinear Models, *Economics Letters*, Vol. 54, pp. 119-126.

Griffin, J.M. and Gregory, P.R. (1976), An Intercountry Translog Model of Energy Substitution Responses, *American Economic Review*, Vol. 66, No. 5, pp. 845-857.

Hamermesh, Daniel S. (1993), *Labor Demand*, Princeton University Press, Princeton.

Hulten, Charles (1986), Short Run and Long Run Cost Functions and the Measurement of Efficiency Change, *Journal of Econometrics*, Vol. 33, No. 1/2 (October-November), pp. 31-50.

Morrison, Catherine (1986), Productivity Measurement with Nonstatic Expectations and Varying Capacity Utilization: An Integrated Approach, *Journal of Econometrics*, Vol. 33, No.1/2, (October-November), pp. 51-74.

Morrison, Catherine (1988), Subequilibrium in the North American Steel Industries: A Study of Short Run Biases From Regulation and Utilisation Fluctuations, *The Economic Journal*, Vol. 98, pp. 390-411.

Morrison, Catherine (1989), Unravelling the Productivity Growth Slowdown in the U.S., Canada and Japan: The Effects of Subequilibrium, Scale Economies and Markups, *National Bureau of Economic Research Working Paper*, No. 2993, June.

Morrison, Catherine (1993), *A Microeconomic Approach to the Measurement of Economic Performance*, Springer-Verlag, New York.

Pagan, Adrian (1984), Econometric Issues in the Analysis of Regressions with Generated Regressors, *International Economic Review*, Vol. 25 (February), pp. 221-247.

Quandt, Richard E. and Rosen, Harvey S. (1988), *The Conflict Between Equilibrium and Disequilibrium Theories: The Case of the U.S. Labor Market*, W.E. Upjohn Institute for Employment Research, Kalamazoo, Michigan.

Truett, Lila and Truett, Dale B. (1996), A Cost Function Analysis of the Australian Transportation Equipment Industry, *The Australian Economic Review*, 4th Quarter, pp. 367-378.

Watts, Geof and Quiggin, John (1984), A Note on the Use of a Logarithmic Time Trend, *Review of Marketing and Agricultural Economics*, Vol, 52, No. 2 (August), pp. 91-99.

8 Pass-Through Elasticities for Production Costs and Competing Foreign Prices: Evidence from Manufacturing Prices in Seven Countries

Harry Bloch and
Michael Olive

I. INTRODUCTION

Growth in international trade increases the exposure of domestic producers to their foreign competitors in both the domestic and export markets. When movements in prices set by these foreign competitors diverge from the movement of domestic costs, domestic producers are faced with a choice whether to follow changes in their own costs or changes in competing foreign prices (or to follow neither) in setting their own prices. This paper provides estimates of the influence of both production costs and prices of competing foreign products on pricing by manufacturing firms in seven industrialized countries (Canada, Germany, Japan, Korea, Sweden, United Kingdom and United States) over the period 1980 to 1990.

The idea that producers follow their own costs in setting prices is the basis of the concept of mark-up pricing. In their seminal study, Hall and Hitch (1939) find that most firms set prices relative to some notion of average cost and a reasonable mark-up to cover profits. Hall and Hitch suggest that this indicates firms are not profit maximizers, but Machlup (1946) demonstrates the formal equivalence of mark-up pricing and profit maximization. Empirical studies of pricing behavior in manufacturing have long recognized the influence of production costs on pricing (see, for example, Eckstein and Fromm (1968) for the United States, and Coutts, Godley and Nordhaus (1978) for the United Kingdom).

Alternatively, the idea that the price set by domestic producers follows the price of competing foreign product is embodied in the law of one price. Commodity arbitrage under the law ensures that undifferentiated product prices do not differ across countries, once transport costs and trade barriers are taken into account. The assumption of both effective arbitrage and a lack of differentiation between domestic and foreign product varieties have been subject to criticism. Using disaggregated data that are matched across the United States, Germany and Japan, Ceglowski (1994) tests strong (in levels) and weak (in rates of change) versions of the law of one price. She finds little long-run support for the law of one price, a result which is consistent with other studies (see Goldstein and Khan (1985) for a review). Despite this, the law of one price is widely used in the analysis of international trade, foreign exchange rate determination and stabilization policy.

In the last decade, there has been an increased interest in the effects of imperfect competition on pricing behavior in open economies. Prices of exports and imports, rather than pricing for the domestic market, has received most of the attention.[63] Our work extends the modest amount of research into the impact of foreign competing prices on domestic pricing in imperfectly competitive markets. Earlier studies include Hazledine (1980) as well as Kardasz and Stollery (1988) for Canada, Feinberg (1986) for Germany, Feinberg (1989) as well as Feinberg and Kaplan (1992) for the United States, and Bloch and Olive (1996) for Australia.

Section II outlines equations for determining prices using mark-up pricing, the law of one price and an oligopoly model. The oligopoly pricing equation is derived from a model with generalized Bertrand conjectures for the price responses from domestic and foreign rivals. Section III describes the data, Section IV outlines and discusses the results, and Section V presents the conclusions.

II. PRICING EQUATIONS

In this section, pricing equations are presented for mark-up pricing, the law of one price and an oligopoly model (with and without an explicit role for market structure in influencing pricing). Pass-through elasticities for both production cost and competing foreign price are derived for each equation. It is then shown that all four of the equations can be nested within an encompassing equation in terms of the rates of change of variables. Restrictions on the coefficients of the encompassing equation for testing each of the underlying pricing hypotheses are derived along with an expression for using estimates of the coefficients in calculating pass-through elasticities.

---

[63] Menon (1995) tabulates 43 studies of pricing behavior with international trade. Of these, only six deal wholly or partially with domestic pricing. The remainder deal exclusively with either export or import prices.

Mark-up pricing is taken to imply that the mark-up factor remains constant. In this case, the rate of change in domestic price is identically equal to the rate of change in cost as follows:

$$p_{dk} = c_{dk} \qquad (1)$$

where p_{dk} is the rate of change in domestic price in the kth industry and c_{dk} is the corresponding rate of change in domestic direct unit cost. In equation (1) there is no intercept term and the rate of change in domestic direct unit cost has a constant coefficient equal to one. The implied pass-through elasticity for production cost is one, while the corresponding pass-through elasticity for competing foreign price is zero.

The law of one price in its relative form implies equality between the rate in change of domestic price and the rate of change in foreign competing price, so that

$$p_{dk} = p_{fk} \qquad (2)$$

where p_{fk} is the rate of change in foreign price for product that competes with that of the kth domestic industry. In equation (2) there is no intercept term and the rate of change in foreign competing product price has a constant coefficient equal to one. The implied pass-through elasticity for competing foreign price is one, while the corresponding pass-through elasticity for production cost is zero.

Dornbusch (1987) considers the joint determination of domestic and foreign competing prices in a variety of models of partial equilibrium under imperfect competition. He finds that domestic pricing depends on assumptions concerning the degree of substitutability between products and the degree of competition both at home and abroad. In each model considered, he finds that the equilibrium response of domestic price to a change in the exchange rate involves a pass-through elasticity of between zero and one (the percentage change in domestic price is in the same direction but smaller in magnitude than the percentage change in the exchange rate). Dornbusch concludes, therefore, that neither the law of one price nor fixed mark-up pricing is consistent with equilibrium pricing under imperfect competition.

Bloch (1992) considers a model of imperfect competition with differentiated products in which the perceived elasticity of demand facing a domestic producer depends on its conjectures concerning the pricing responses of foreign and domestic rivals. The rate of domestic price change in equilibrium is found to be a linear homogeneous function of the rate of change in domestic production cost and the rate of change in the price of competing foreign product as follows:

$$p_{dk} = \alpha_1 c_{dk} + \alpha_2 p_{fk} \tag{3}$$

The coefficients, α_1 and α_2, in (3) provide direct estimates of the pass-through elasticity for production cost and foreign competing price, respectively. They are each non-negative in the case of a number of different functional forms for product demand and sum to one under special conditions.[64]

Market structure can affect the α coefficients in (3) through altering the magnitude of a firm's perceived price elasticity of demand. In Appendix 1, the absolute value of the perceived demand elasticity is shown have a positive effect on α_1 and a negative effect on α_2. More concentrated market structures are generally associated with less elastic perceived demand curves. We use the inverse of the number of enterprises in a domestic industry as a measure of domestic market concentration in the regression estimates below.[65]

Assuming a linear relationship between the inverse of the number of firms and each of the coefficients in (3), we have

$$p_{dk} = \left(\beta_{1k} + \beta_{2k}\frac{1}{m_{dk}}\right) c_{dk} + \left(\beta_{3k} + \beta_{4k}\frac{1}{m_{dk}}\right) p_{fk} \tag{4}$$

where m_{dk} equals the number of firms in the kth domestic industry. The restrictions on the coefficients in equation (4) implied by the discussion above are that $\beta_{2k} < 0$ and $\beta_{4k} > 0$, and that the terms in parentheses are each less than or equal to one and greater than or equal

---

[64] Bloch (1992) shows that both coefficients are positive for either a linear or semi-logarithmic form of the demand function, but that the coefficient of domestic production cost is one and the coefficient of foreign price is zero for a double-logarithmic demand function. The value of the sum of the coefficients is one for functional forms other than double log, provided that the rate of change in the price elasticity of demand is homogeneous of degree zero in the rates of change of prices for the group of domestic and foreign products included in the industry.

[65] The use of the inverse of the number of firms as a measure of concentration has the disadvantage of not taking firm inequality into consideration, unlike the Herfindahl index (each firm's share of industry turnover squared, then summed over the whole industry) and the n-firm concentration ratio (the share of industry turnover attributable to the top n firms). However, it can be shown that Herfindahl index and the n-firm concentration ratio are a function of the inverse of the number of firms, as well as firm inequality. In addition, when all firms are of the same size in an industry, and the one-firm concentration ratio is considered, all three measures are equivalent. In practice, there is a high level of correlation between all three measures, although these differences may still be important empirically (Hay and Morris, 1991, p. 215).

to zero. There are no particular restrictions imposed on the coefficients, β_{1k} and β_{3k}, separately. As with equations (1) through (3), there is no constant term. The implied pass-through elasticity for production cost is increasing with the number of firms in the domestic industry, while the corresponding elasticity for competing foreign price is decreasing with the number of firms.

We use data for cross sections of industries in estimating an encompassing pricing equation for each of seven countries, assuming that the estimated coefficients in the equations are equal across industries. Such uniformity is not required for the pricing equations in (3) or (4), so that extra inflexibility is imposed. However, this requirement has the effect of making (3) and (4) more comparable to (1) and (2) for predictive and policy purposes. With uniform coefficients across industries, the only industry-specific information necessary for determining pass-through elasticities is the number of domestic firms. We allow for other influences on domestic price inflation, not associated with the above pricing equations, by including a constant term in our estimating equations.[66] The resulting equation is of the following form:

$$p_{dk} = \beta_0 + \left(\beta_1 + \beta_2 \frac{1}{m_{dk}}\right) c_{dk} + \left(\beta_3 + \beta_4 \frac{1}{m_{dk}}\right) p_{fk} \qquad (5)$$

The relationship in (5) encompasses the relationships in each of the preceding equations. To obtain any of the preceding equations, we need $\beta_0 = 0$. This is the only restriction required to obtain (4). A further requirement to obtain (3) is that $\beta_2 = 0$ and $\beta_4 = 0$. This provides a relationship consistent with imperfect competition, but without any role for the number of firms as an influence on conjectural elasticities. The relationship for the law of one price in (2) obtains, when $\beta_1 = 0$ and $\beta_3 = 1$ and in addition to $\beta_0 = \beta_2 = \beta_4 = 0$. Finally, to obtain the fixed mark-up relationship in (1), the required values are $\beta_1 = 1$ and $\beta_3 = 0$, along with $\beta_0 = \beta_2 = \beta_4 = 0$.

Taking the derivatives of (5) with respect to the rate of change in cost and the rate of change in foreign price, gives the following expressions for the pass-through elasticities:

---

[66] Inclusion of a constant term provides a crude test for misspecification in that it captures the portion of the mean value of the dependent variable that is not related to the explanatory variables. The influence of omitted variables also leads to bias in the estimated coefficients of the included variables, to the extent that the omitted variables are correlated with the included variables.

$$\theta_{cdk} = \partial p_{dk} / \partial c_{dk} = \beta_1 + \beta_2 \frac{1}{m_{dk}}$$

$$\theta_{pfk} = \partial p_{dk} / \partial p_{fk} = \beta_3 + \beta_4 \frac{1}{m_{dk}} \tag{6}$$

In the general case, the elasticities calculated from the parameter estimates of the encompassing equation depend on market structure as measured by the number of firms. However, as noted above, only the oligopoly model with conjectures dependent on market structure leads to specific predictions concerning the direction of impact of the number of firms, positive for the cost elasticity and negative for the foreign price elasticity. There is no role for the number of firms to alter pass-through elasticities in the fixed mark-up model, equation (1), the law of one price, equation (2), or the general model of imperfect competition, equation (3).

III. DATA

A difficulty researchers have with cross-country studies is finding data that are comparable. The United Nations Industrial Development Organization (UNIDO) provides manufacturing data at the three-digit International Standard Industrial Classification (ISIC) for a large number of countries. We use data for each of seven countries, each with complete data for twenty-four of the three-digit ISIC manufacturing industries (countries and industries are listed in the data appendix).[67] Included in the group of countries are the G7 countries, except France and Italy are excluded due to incomplete information. We add Korea and Sweden to the sample as major industrial countries for which data are available in all the sample industries.

The price and cost change measures used in our estimates are each average annual rates of change for the decade, 1980 through 1990. We use average changes over a lengthy period to isolate a long-run pricing

---

[67] Although UNIDO provides information on 28 industries, data on the Tobacco, Beverages, Petroleum Refineries, and Miscellaneous Petroleum and Coal Products industries are considered unreliable due to varying methods of accounting for excise taxes across countries. Sensitivity testing indicates that these four industries do have effects that improve the performance of the oligopoly model. However, as it is not possible to tell if this is due to the high level of concentration in these industries or to the data being unreliable, they are not included in the reported results.

Table 8.1

Regressions for the Rate of Domestic Price Change in Seven Countries, Each with 24 Three Digit ISIC Industries, 1980 to 1990.

		Estimated coefficient of					
				Inverse of the Number of Enterprises multiplied by			
	Const.	Rate of Change in Unit Direct Costs	Rate of Change in Foreign Price	Rate of Change in Unit Direct Costs	Rate of Change in Foreign Price	R^2	Hausman Test[#] (probability values)
Combined Countries	0.010** (7.19)	0.970** (46.53)	-0.084** (-3.27)	-38.372* (-2.42)	20.755** (2.86)	0.944	
Canada	0.004 (1.71)	1.039** (23.88)	-0.113 (-1.58)	-46.184** (-7.88)	34.994** (6.69)	0.967	0.364
Germany	0.021** (5.44)	0.905**a (7.624)	-0.287 (-1.75)	-93.586** (-2.83)	85.509 (1.66)	0.804	0.954
Japan	0.014** (3.95)	0.923** (36.60)	-0.194** (-2.73)	32.531 (0.37)	212.613 (1.50)	0.969	0.133
Korea	0.005 (1.53)	1.011** (22.40)	0.062 (0.62)	-19.10 (-1.35)	8.41 (0.36)	0.981	1.000
Sweden	0.012** (5.47)	0.914** (19.83)	-0.104 (-1.45)	-17.745** (-3.08)	11.909** (3.62)	0.956	0.310
United Kingdom	0.008** (3.46)	0.817** (17.71)	-0.012 (-0.22)	163.051** (3.89)	-49.437 (-1.85)	0.949	0.379
United States	0.009** (3.69)	1.007** (30.87)	-0.110** (-2.80)	-331.428** (-4.38)	208.076** (4.41)	0.958	0.522

Figures in parentheses are White heteroscedasticity-consistent t-statistics.
** indicates if the coefficient is statistically different from zero, using a two-tailed t test at the 1% level of significance. and * indicates if the coefficient is statistically different from zero, using a two-tailed t test at the 5% level of significance.
'a' indicates if the "rate of change in unit direct cost" coefficient is not statistically different from one, using a two-tailed t test at the 5% level of significance.
The Hausman test follows a chi-square distribution, with 5 degrees of freedom. The critical value is 9.236 at the 10% level of significance.

relationship from the possible slow adjustment of prices.[68] The price measure for each country is the average annual rate of change by industry of the implicit price index for industrial production, while the foreign competing price measure is the average of corresponding measures for the same industry in all other countries (after adjusting each measure for changes in foreign exchange rates).[69] Our cost measure is the average annual rate of change in wage and materials costs per unit of industrial production. Specific details of series construction are contained in the Data Appendix.

UNIDO provides data on the number of establishments by industry, which we use as an approximation to the number of firms.[70] In each country, the number of establishments is for 1985, except for the United States, where it is for 1992. In this latter case, establishments data, at the 3 digit ISIC level, are taken from the OECD, *Industrial Structure Statistics, 1993*.

IV. RESULTS

Table 8.1 presents the results of estimating regressions in the form of the encompassing equation, (5), using data for our sample of 24 industries. Separate results are reported for each of the seven industrial countries, using seemingly unrelated regression estimation (SURE). The use of SURE allows for the possibility that the disturbances affecting individual industries are related across countries. Also presented are results for all countries combined (Combined Countries), using ordinary least squares.

---

[68] Many studies of industrial pricing focus on the process of price adjustment or on the influence of cyclical factors on pricing. Our concern is to distinguish the separate influences of domestic production costs and foreign prices, while allowing these influences to vary with domestic market structure. Cross-section data for average rates of change over a lengthy period are chosen for this purpose.

[69] Our price measures make no allowance for differences between prices charged in the domestic market and prices charged in foreign markets. This is a limitation of the data set used in the study. The influences of trade barriers and of price discrimination across markets are thereby excluded from the measure of the price of competing foreign products. Only if these influences have a constant proportional impact over time, will our measure of the rate of change of foreign competing prices be without error.

[70] For example, the correlation between the inverse number of establishments and the inverse number of enterprises in Australian manufacturing industry, taken at the 3-digit ASIC (Australian Standard Industrial Classification) level, is 0.987 (Australian Bureau of Statistics, *Census of Manufacturing and Electricity and Gas Establishments, Industry Concentration Statistics, Australia, 1986-87*). For 38 leading industries in Canada the correlation is 0.950 (*1985 Canada Yearbook*).

These results are presented for illustrative purposes only, as the hypothesis that the estimated coefficients are uniform across countries is rejected at the one percent significance level.[71] All standard errors in Table 8.1 are adjusted for heteroscedasticity, using the White method as given by *TSP 4.3* (see Hall (1995)).

As discussed at the end of Section II, each of the pricing equations, (1) through (4), is nested within our encompassing equation for a specific set of linear restrictions on the estimated coefficients. We test each of these restrictions using an F-statistic test (see Judge, *et al.* (1988, pp. 456-462)). All restrictions are rejected at the five percent significance level in every country, except for Canada and Korea. In both Canada and Korea the only restriction accepted is that for equation (4), the pricing equation for the oligopoly model version that includes a role for market structure.[72]

Cost changes play a dominant role in the determination of domestic prices in every country according to the regression results in Table 8.1. The coefficient for the rate of change in unit direct cost is significantly different from zero at the one percent significance level using a two-tailed t-test in every country and in the Combined Countries regression. Further, the coefficient of the cost change variable is not significantly different from one in the cases of Canada, Germany, Korea, Sweden, the United States and Combined Countries, suggesting a proportional relation as predicted by the fixed mark-up model. However, as noted above, the full set of restrictions associated with the fixed mark-up model is rejected for each of these countries as well as Japan and the United Kingdom, as the cost change variable alone does not adequately explain changes in domestic prices.

The coefficient for the rate of change in foreign price is significantly negative for Japan, the United States and Combined Countries, and not significantly different from zero for all other countries. These results are clearly inconsistent with the law of one price, so that rejection of this pricing model in the F-tests on linear restrictions is hardly surprising.

In Canada, Sweden, the United States and Combined Countries, the coefficient for the inverse of the number of establishments multiplied by the rate of change in unit direct cost (cost cross-variable) is negative

---

[71] The F-statistic for the restriction that the coefficients of each of the explanatory variables is the same in each country is 100.1, the appropriate critical value for the one percent significance level is $F_{24,133} = 1.97$.

[72] The restrictions for the general model of imperfect competition given in equation (3) are rejected at the five percent significance level for Korea and at the one percent significance level for Canada. In addition, the restriction that the constant term is zero can not be rejected at the five percent significance level in either country. Thus, the restrictions associated with equation (4) are accepted for both countries, but the restrictions for equation (3) are accepted in neither country.

and significantly different from zero, while the coefficient for the inverse of the number of establishments multiplied by the rate of change in foreign price (foreign price cross-variable) is positive and significantly different from zero. For these countries, the rate of change in foreign price becomes increasingly important, and the rate of change in unit direct cost becomes decreasingly important, as the number of establishments in an industry becomes smaller, and vice versa. This outcome is consistent with the predictions of the oligopoly model and helps to explain the failure to accept restrictions associated with the simple rule-of-thumb relationship suggested by the fixed mark-up model. Of the other four countries, Germany has the same cross-variable signs as the previous countries but only the cost cross-variable is significantly different from zero. Neither of the cross-variables is significantly different from zero in the cases of Japan and Korea. The United Kingdom has opposite signs, but only the cost cross-variable is significantly different from zero.

So far it has been assumed that the rate of change in foreign price is exogenous and, therefore, unaffected by the rate of change in domestic price. The Hausman specification test is used to test this hypothesis, with the results given in Table 8.1.[73] For all countries the Chi-squared test statistic was not significant at the ten percent level, giving us good statistical grounds for believing that foreign prices are exogenous.

The results in Table 8.1 indicate that pass-through elasticities for both production cost and foreign competing price generally depend on market structure. The potential magnitude of the effect of market structure is shown in Table 8.2. Elasticities in Table 8.2 are calculated from the elasticity formulae in (6) for both the maximum and minimum number of establishments in any industry for each country. In the cases of Canada, Sweden and the United States, the pass-through elasticity for production cost falls by .93, .83 and .67, respectively, when the number of establishments is at a minimum rather than maximum. The corresponding increases in the pass-through elasticity for foreign competing are .71, .56, and .42, respectively. Averaged over the seven countries, between the maximum and minimum number of establishments there is a .40 reduction in the cost pass-through elasticity and a .33 increase in the foreign price pass-through elasticity.

---

[73] The method used for calculating the Hausman specification test is that shown in Hall (1995, p. 69). Ordinary least squares are used as the unbiased and efficient estimation method under the null hypothesis, while instrumental variable estimation is used as the method for the alternative hypothesis. A weighted average of the rate of change in foreign direct unit costs is used as the instrumental variable for the rate of change in foreign price.

Table 8.2

Production Cost and Competing Foreign Price Pass-Through Elasticities for the Minimum and Maximum Industry Establishment Numbers in Each Country

		Number of Industry Establishments	Pass-Through Elasticity of	
			Production Cost	Competing Foreign Price
Canada				
	Min.	49	0.096	0.601
	Max.	5443	1.031	-0.107
Germany				
	Min.	163	0.331	0.238
	Max.	5421	0.888	-0.271
Japan				
	Min.	1344	0.947	-0.036
	Max.	51607	0.924	-0.190
Korea				
	Min.	221	0.925	0.100
	Max.	6118	1.008	0.063
Sweden				
	Min.	21	0.069	0.463
	Max.	1547	0.903	-0.096
United Kingdom				
	Min.	600	1.089	-0.094
	Max.	22025	0.824	-0.014
United States				
	Min.	492	0.333	0.313
	Max.	65476	1.002	-0.107

V. CONCLUSION

We derive pricing equations for a fixed mark-up model, the law of one price and two versions of an oligopoly pricing model (with and without an explicit role for market structure). An encompassing equation is then used to estimate pricing relationships for each of seven industrialized countries and test the linear restriction sets implied by each of the pricing models. Examining the results shows that the coefficients in the equations differ significantly across countries. However, in each country, simple rules of thumb associated with fixed mark-up pricing and the law of one price are rejected at the one percent significance level. This failure should serve as a salutary caution against assuming these simple pricing rules for reasons of convenience or approximation in the economic analysis of modern open economies.

The oligopoly pricing model provides an adequate explanation for pricing in only two countries, Canada and Korea, with the concentration cross-variables statistically significant in only the first country.[74] However, there are significant coefficients for at least one concentration cross-variable in most countries. In Canada, Germany, Sweden and the United States, the impact of industry concentration is large enough to reduce the estimated pass-through elasticity for production cost from close to one to under one half, comparing the industry with lowest concentration in the sample to the industry with the highest concentration. There are corresponding increases in the pass-through elasticity for foreign competing price from slightly negative to between a positive one quarter and one half.

Our results show that domestic cost has the dominant influence on pricing in competitively structured industries in all countries, but that foreign influences generally play an increasing role as domestic concentration rises. We demonstrate that industry characteristics need to be considered in analyses of price determination in the manufacturing industries of modern economies. This should provide encouragement to the further development of open-economy models of oligopoly pricing, such as including industry characteristics besides concentration, as well as encouraging development of more refined and extensive comparable measures of market structure.

---

[74] The strength of the Canadian results is not surprising given that the successful inclusion of market structure variables in the empirical analysis of manufacturing prices in Canada has a long tradition (see, for example, Bloch (1974), Hazledine (1980) and Kardasz and Stollery (1988)), which is unparalleled in other countries.

Appendix 8.1

The model presented here follows Bloch (1992). Assuming a differentiated product market and constant marginal cost, the short-run profit function is given by

$$\pi_i = (p_i - c_i) * y_i (p_i, p_1, ..., p_j, ..., p_m) \qquad (A1)$$

where π_i, p_i, c_i, and y_i, are the ith firm's profit, product price, product marginal cost and output, respectively, and the p_j (where j=1,..,m and j≠ i) are the product prices of competing firms. Marginal cost and direct unit cost (i.e. average cost of wages and raw materials) are equal for the firm, and its level of output is a positive function of the price of competing product and a negative function of its own product price.

Differentiating the above profit function with respect to the ith firm's product price to obtain the first-order conditions for profit maximization and rearranging, gives the following pricing equation for a non-collusive oligopolist:

$$p_i = \frac{c_i}{\left(1 + \frac{1}{\eta_i}\right)} \text{ and } -\infty < \eta_i < -1 \qquad (A2)$$

where η_i is the perceived elasticity of demand. Taking rates of change gives

$$p_i = c_i + h_i * \left(\frac{1}{1 + \eta_i}\right) \qquad (A3)$$

where p_i, c_i and h_i are the ith firm's product price, marginal cost and perceived elasticity of demand expressed as rates of change.

Using a first-order approximation to a Taylor expansion, the rate of change of the ith firm's perceived elasticity of demand is represented as the following linear function:

$$h_i = a_i p_i + \sum_{j \neq 1} b_{ij} p_j \qquad (A4)$$

where p_j is the rate of change of the jth competing product price. The coefficients, a_i and the b_{ij} are all constant with respect to time and determined by the demand function. To satisfy stability and the intuitive condition of a non-negative effect of competing price changes on the profit-maximizing price in (A3), we need $a_i \geq 0$ and $b_{ij} \leq 0$. Further, if (A4) is homogeneous of degree zero in the rates of change of prices of the product and its close substitutes, we have $a_i = -\sum_{j \neq i} b_{ij}$ and the perceived price elasticity of demand is unaffected by equal changes in the price of all products among the group of close substitutes.

Substituting equation (A4) into equation (A3) and solving for the compound rate of change of the ith firm's own price results in the following expression:

$$p_i = c_i * \frac{(1 + \eta_i)}{(1 + \eta_i - a_i)} + \sum_{j \neq i} p_j * \frac{b_{ij}}{(1 + \eta_i - a_i)} \quad (A5)$$

Here, the coefficients of the cost and competing price terms are both non-negative under the assumptions given with (A4). Further, the coefficients sum to one under the condition of homogeneity of degree zero for (A4), provided that the competing prices all change at the same rate.

If foreign firms sell into the domestic market, equation (A5) can be expressed as follows:

$$p_i = c_i * \frac{(1 + \eta_i)}{(1 + \eta_i - a_i)} + \sum_{\substack{j \in d \\ j \neq i}} p_j * \frac{b_{ij}}{(1 + h_i - a_i)} + \sum_{j \in f} p_j * \frac{b_{ij}}{(1 + \eta_i - a_i)} \quad (A6)$$

where $j \in d$ and $j \in f$ indicate that the competing prices relate to domestic product and foreign product, respectively. Weighting the ith firm's pricing equation by its share in the value of domestic industry shipments, then summing over the domestic industry gives the following domestic industry pricing equation:

$$p_d = c_d * \frac{(1 + \alpha \eta_d)}{(1 + \eta_d - a_d - b_d)} + p_f * \frac{b_f}{(1 + \eta_d - a_d - b_d)} \quad (A7)$$

where the d subscript indicates a weighted average over domestic products, the f subscript indicates a weighted average over foreign products, and α is a weighting correction. The terms multiplying both the cost change and foreign price change are non-negative under the assumptions given with (A4). Further, if (A4) is homogeneous of degree zero, and ignoring the effects of weighting, the coefficients of cost change and competing foreign price change in (A7) sum to one. This is basis for the special case restriction on the coefficients of (3) referred to in the text above.

As the average perceived elasticity of demand, η_d, in (A7) becomes less elastic, the coefficient for the average compound rate of domestic cost change becomes smaller and the coefficient for the compound rate of change of the average price for competing foreign product becomes larger. Assuming that the perceived elasticity of demand is a positive function of concentration, equation (A7) provides the basis for the relationship in (4) in the text above.

Data Appendix

List of Countries and Industries

Countries:

Australia	Japan	South Africa
Canada	Korea	Sweden
Denmark	Malaysia	Taiwan
Germany	Netherlands	Thailand
Hong Kong	New Zealand	United Kingdom
India	Norway	United States
Italy	Singapore	

Industries:

Food Products	(311)
Wearing Apparel, except Footwear	(322)
Leather Products	(323)
Footwear, except Rubber or Plastic	(324)
Wood Products, Except Furniture	(331)
Furniture, except Metal	(332)
Paper and Products	(341)
Printing and Publishing	(342)
Industrial Chemicals	(351)
Other Chemicals	(352)
Rubber Products	(355)
Plastic Products	(356)
Pottery, China, Earthenware	(361)
Glass and Products	(362)
Other Non-Metallic Mineral Products	(369)
Iron and Steel	(371)
Non-Ferrous Metals	(372)
Fabricated Metal Products	(381)
Machinery, except Electrical	(382)
Machinery, Electrical	(383)
Transport Equipment	(384)
Professional and Scientific Equipment	(385)
Other Manufacturing Products	(390)

UNIDO (United Nations Industrial Development Organization) three-digit ISIC (International Standard Industrial Classification) data are used in constructing series for the compound rate of change in domestic industry product price, the compound rate of change in domestic industry product cost, the compound rate of change in foreign industry product price, and the number of establishments in each industry (except in the case of US establishments). While seven countries are analyzed in the results section, information on 20 countries is used to construct the compound rate of change in foreign industry product price. The countries and industry categories are identified in table DA1. Exchange rate data are taken from Penn World Tables.

p_d is the compound rate of change in domestic industry product price. Domestic price indexes are constructed by dividing industry nominal gross output by an index of production (base year, 1980) and converting to $US. The compound rate of change is calculated by dividing the 1990 index value by the 1980 index value, taking the tenth root, then deducting one.

c_d is the compound rate of change in domestic industry cost. Domestic cost indexes are constructed by adding an industry's nominal gross output and wages and salaries, deducting the industry's value added, and then dividing this total by an index of production (base year, 1980) and converting to $US. The compound rate of change is calculated by dividing the 1990 index value by the 1980 index value, taking the tenth root, then deducting one.

p_f is the compound rate of change in competing foreign industry product price. A weighted average of all the $p_d + 1$ from competing foreign industries, taken annually, is used to find a geometric average across the ten year period. Deducting one gives the compound rate of change. This method is preferred as it allows for missing observations. The weights are each country's 1985 industry shares of world gross output (in $US), excluding output in the relevant domestic economy.

m_d is the number of industry establishments in 1985, except for the United States, where it is the number of industry establishments in 1992. Collection of this data is consistent within countries, but not across all countries (Canada, Japan and US, include all enterprises in an industry; Korea and Sweden include enterprises with 5 or more employees; and Germany and the UK include enterprises with 20 or more employees).

REFERENCES

Bloch, Harry (1974), Prices, Costs and Profits in Canadian Manufacturing: The Influence of Tariffs and Concentration, *Canadian Journal of Economics*, 7, pp. 594-610.

Bloch, Harry (1992), Pricing in Australian Manufacturing, *The Economic Record*, 68, pp. 365-376.

Bloch, Harry and Olive, Michael (1996), Can Simple Rules Explain Pricing in Australian Manufacturing?, *Australian Economic Papers*, 35, pp. 1-19.

Ceglowski, Janet (1994), The Law of One Price Revisited: New Evidence on the Behavior of International Prices, *Economic Inquiry*, 32, pp. 407-418.

Coutts, Kenneth, Godley, Wynne and Nordhaus, William (1978), *Industrial Pricing in the United Kingdom*, Cambridge University Press, Cambridge.

Dornbusch, Rudiger (1987), Exchange Rates and Prices, *American Economic Review*, 77, pp. 93-106.

Eckstein, Otto and Fromm, Gary (1968), The Price Equation, *American Economic Review*, 58, pp. 1158-83.

Feinberg, Robert M. (1986), The Interaction of Foreign Exchange and Market Power Effects on German Domestic Prices, *The Journal of Industrial Economics*, 35, pp. 61-70.

Feinberg, Robert M. (1989), The Effects of Foreign Exchange Movements on U.S. Domestic Prices, *Review of Economics and Statistics*, 71, pp. 505-511.

Feinberg, Robert M. and Kaplan, Seth (1992), The Response of Domestic Prices to Expected Exchange Rates, *Journal of Business*, 65, pp. 267-280.

Goldstein, Morris and Khan, Mohsin S. (1985), Income and Price Effects in Foreign Trade, in Jones, R.W. and Kenen, P.B. (ed), *Handbook of International Economics*, North Holland, Amsterdam, pp. 1041-1105.

Hall, Bronwyn H. (1995), *TSP User's Guide: Version 4.3*, TSP International, Palo Alto.

Hall, R. and Hitch, C. (1939), Price Theory and Business Behaviour, *Oxford Economic Papers*, 2, pp. 12-45.

Hay, Donald A. and Morris, Derek J. (1991), *Industrial Economics and Organization*, Oxford University Press, New York.

Hazledine, Tim (1980), Testing Two Models of Pricing and Protection with Canada/United States Data, *Journal of Industrial Economics*, 29, pp. 145-154.

Judge, George G., Hill, R. Carter, Griffiths, William E., Lütkepohl, Helmet, and Lee, Tsoung-Chao (1988), *Introduction to the Theory and Practice of Econometrics*, Wiley and Sons, New York.

Kardasz, Stanley W. and Stollery, Kenneth (1988), Price Formation in Canadian Manufacturing Industries, *Applied Economics*, 20, pp. 473-483.

Machlup, Fritz (1946), Marginal Analysis and Empirical Research, *American Economic Review*, 36, pp. 519-554.

Menon, Jayant (1995), Exchange Rate Pass-through, *Journal of Economic Surveys*, 9, pp. 197-231.

Sawyer, Malcolm C (1983), *Business Pricing and Inflation*, Macmillan Press, London.

9 Non-Linear Costs and Returns to Scale: Some Disaggregate Results

Erkin I. Bairam

I. INTRODUCTION

This short paper aims at estimating appropriate cost functions and analyzing the scale elasticities in 58 big companies or corporations which trade on the New York Stock Exchange. For this purpose time-series data for the period 1975-92 were used and new cost functions were estimated. In section II the cost function which was used is specified and its properties are discussed. Section III examines the results obtained and summarises the conclusions drawn.

II. THE COST FUNCTION

Econometric applications of the cost function are often variants of the general type:

$$C_{it} = f(t, Q_{it}) \tag{1}$$

where C_{it} and Q_{it} are the total output and cost of firm i in period t. This general function is very often assumed to be homogeneous and, hence, assumed to be a non-variable returns to scale function (see Chapter 1). The time variable is included in order to allow for effects of quality changes over time and it is assumed $\partial C_{it}/\partial t \leq 0$. Therefore, if cross section data are used for estimation purposes, t is zero. However, even when t = 0, equation (1) cannot be estimated unless an explicit assumption is made about the functional relationship between C_{it} and Q_{it}. In practice it is usually assumed that this relationship is either linear or quadratic. However, one should object to this approach as its implementation requires one to specify *a priori* a particular functional form for the firm's cost (and production) processes (see Chapters 1 and 2). This raises the important issue as to whether it is possible to discriminate among the various functional forms and, thus, to choose the one that best represents the given technology – see Khaled (1977), Berndt and Khaled (1979), Bairam (1991a, 1991b and 1994).

Here, in order to eliminate the *a priori* assumption about the functional form, the following Box-Cox function will be used:

$$[(C_{it}^{\lambda_i}-1)/\lambda_i] = \alpha_{0i} + \alpha_{1i}t + \beta_i [(Q_{it}^{\lambda_i}-1)/\lambda_i] \qquad (2)$$

where $\infty^- \leq \lambda_i \leq \infty^+$; $\alpha_{0i}, \beta_i \geq 0$ and $\alpha_{1i} \leq 0$.

Different values of λ_i will lead to various well-known functional forms. For example when $\lambda_i = 1$, equation (2) will yield the linear function.

This specification yields the following total cost elasticity, ε_{cit}:

$$\varepsilon_{cit} = (dC_{it}/C_{it}/dQ_{it}/Q_{it})$$

$$= \beta_i (Q_{it}/C_{it})^{\lambda_i}$$

$$= \beta_i (C_{it}/Q_{it})^{-\lambda_i} \qquad (3)$$

where (C_{it}/Q_{it}) is obviously the average cost.

It is important to note that unless $\lambda_i = 0$ (i.e. log-linear functional form) the cost elasticity, ε_{cit}, is **variable**. If and only if $\lambda_i = 0$ (i.e homogeneous functional form), $\varepsilon_{cit} = \beta_i$ and constant. It is also important to note that since:

$$\varepsilon_{cit} = 1/\varepsilon_{it} \qquad (4)$$

the elasticity of cost is the reciprocal of the scale elasticity of production, ε_{it}.[75] Consequently, from the results obtained on cost functions, if one is willing to assume the validity of the duality theorem (see Bairam (1994)), the scale elasticity can be computed using equation (4) and, like (3), ε_{it} could be variable or constant depending upon the value of λ_i.

III. RESULTS AND CONCLUSIONS

The annual time-series(1975-92) data used for estimation purposes cover the 58 biggest 'firms' (companies or corporations) which trade on

---

[75] See Bairam (1994) for proofs and implicit assumptions.

the New York Stock Exchange.[76] All the data used (except the price index) were from the Standard and Poor's *Computstat* data base and were all in 1973 prices.

In order to save space, the full results obtained from the estimation of equation (2) are not reported here. Only the important summary results are given in Tables 9.1, 9.2 and 9.3. However, several key features of the full results should be emphasised.

Firstly, the significance of all estimated equations was excellent. Without any exception, $\bar{R}^2$ is always over 0.98. Secondly all the estimated β_i coefficients are significantly greater than zero at all the conventional test levels. Thirdly, the coefficient on t, α_{1i}, was, in most cases, not significantly different from zero. Last but not least most estimated equations suffered from first order serial-correlation. Consequently, all the estimated equations were corrected for serial-correlation using the maximum likelihood procedure based on Cochrane-Orcutt procedure developed by Beach and MacKinnon (1978). The summary results reported in the Appendix tables are from these re-estimated equations.

Turning to the summary results in the tables, it can be seen they are split into three groups. Table 9.1 consists of the firms which fall into the group $20000 \leq SIC \leq 29999$, which are mainly oil, petro-chemicals and soft drink industries. Table 9.2 covers the firms in the group $30000 \leq SIC\ 39999$, which includes mainly manufacturing industries like electrical, electronic and mechanical engineering. Finally, table 9.3 results are mainly large department stores and food chains – $50000 \leq SIC\ 59999$.

The **average** scale elasticity coefficients ($1/\beta_i$ or $1/\varepsilon_{cit}$) obtained from equation (2) or its restricted version ($\lambda_i = 0$), together with the appropriate likelihood test results which test the hypothesis $H_0: \lambda_i = 0$ (constant elasticity) against $H_0: \lambda_i \neq 0$ (variable elasticity) are reported in the tables. The following main conclusions can be drawn from these results.

1. It can be seen that log-linearity which implies constant elasticity equal to $1/\beta_i$, is accepted for 36 of the firms under consideration. The data for the other 22 firms, however, reject the log-linearity elasticities. Hence, the results in the tables clearly show that the appropriate functional form differs from firm to firm and, thus, the scale elasticity cannot be assumed to be constant all the time.

2. Notwithstanding, whether or not the scale elasticities are variable for

---

[76] The criterion used to decide which firms would be included in the sample was their number of employees in 1992. Firms with more than 5000 employees in 1992 are included in the results.

a given firm, the average elasticities ($1/\beta_i$ or $1/\varepsilon_{cit}$) however, show that the three groups of industries listed in the tables are different when it comes to the degrees of returns to scale. It is clear that all the firms which suffer from significant diseconomies of scale belong to the group $20000 \leq SIC \leq 29999$. That is to say they are oil, petrochemical, chemical and softdrink industries. For example, it is clear that Coca-Cola and Pepsico suffers from huge diseconomies of scale. Likewise oil companies like Amaco, Ashland Oil, Exxon suffer from diseconomies of scale. On the other hand the manufacturing firms from group $30000 \leq SIC \leq 39999$ most have significant economies of scale and none suffers from diseconomies of scale. Constant returns to scale is the norm in the last group, which is dominated by department stores and food chain companies.

Therefore, summing it up, it is very clear that these results suggest that the average degree of returns to scale in a firm is chiefly determined by the technological nature of the industry under consideration and has less to do with efficiency of the firm itself. Consequently these results lend further support to this researcher's belief that the nature of the industry under consideration is very important in determining the economic efficiency of a given firm.[77]

---

[77] See also, for example, Bairam (1987 and 1994).

Table 9.1

Functional Form and Elasticity of Scale, 1975-92: Summary Results, 20000 ≤ SIC ≤ 29999

Name	SIC	χ^2	$\varepsilon = (1/\beta)$	$\varepsilon = (1/\varepsilon_{cit})$
Amco Corp	2911	0.02	0.85	
American Cyanamid Co	2800	13.64		1.01
American Home Prod. Corp	2609	0.46	0.98	
Ashland Oil Inc	2911	0.88	0.84	
Coca Cola Co	2080	106.40		0.83
Colgate-Palmolive Co	2840	0.02	1.09	
Dial Corp	2840	12.56		0.98
DuPont De Menours	2820	0.08	1.08	
Exxon Corp	2911	69.48		0.78
J. Rivers Corp, Virginia	2621	7.06		1.03
Johnson and Johnson	2834	6.31		0.81
Mobil Corp	2911	82.32		0.95
Pepsico Inc	2080	6.70		0.64
Philip Morris Cos Inc	2000	0.16	0.87	
Texaco Inc	2911	0.68	1.01	
Time Warner Inc	2721	1.22	0.75	
Warner-Lambert Co	2834	0.20	0.90	

Notes: $\chi^2 = -2\log\theta$ is the appropriate likelihood ratio used to test the hypothesis $H_0 : \lambda_i = 0$ ($\varepsilon_{cit} = \beta_i$, i.e. constant elasticity). It is asymptotically distributed as χ^2 with one degree of freedom. Therefore, if $\chi^2_{0.05} = 3.84 < -2\log\theta$, H_0 is rejected. ε is the average, 1976-92 income elasticity (for computation of ε, see text).

Table 9.2
Functional Form and Elasticity of Scale, 1975-92:
Summary Results, $30000 \leq SIC \leq 39999$

Name	SIC	χ^2	$\varepsilon = (1/\beta)$	$\varepsilon = (1/\varepsilon_{cit})$
Allied Signal Inc	3724	0.08	1.25	
Black and Decker Corp	3540	2.94	1.02	
Cooper Industries Inc	3640	0.28	1.20	
Corning Inc	3220	9.10		1.18
Dana Corp	3714	3.62	1.20	
Deere and Co	3523	0.02	1.30	
Emerson Electric Co	3823	0.10	1.01	
Ford Motor Co	3711	5.28		1.20
General Electric Co	3600	10.42		1.10
Gillette Co	3420	0.10	0.91	
Grammer Corp	3721	0.01	1.10	
Hewlett Packard Co	3570	1.04	0.95	
IBM	3570	0.02	0.99	
Ingersoll-Rand Co	3560	6.00		1.32
Lockheed Corp	3760	23.22		1.05
M. Marietta Corp	3760	0.04	0.93	
Northern Telecom Ltd	3661	2.73	1.28	
Northop Corp	3721	5.86		0.97
Texas Instr. Inc	3774	2.76	1.11	
Textron Inc	3720	0.16	1.00	
Unisys Corp	3570	0.04	1.15	
United Tech. Corp	3724	3.10	1.14	
Westinghouse Elec. Corp	3510	82.02		1.25

Note: See Table 9.1.

Table 9.3

Functional Form and Elasticity of Scale, 1975-92: Summary Results, $50000 \leq SIC \leq 59999$

Name	SIC	χ^2	$\varepsilon = (1/\beta)$	$\varepsilon = (1/\varepsilon_{cit})$
Alberson Inc.	5411	0.34	1.04	
American Store Co-New	5411	0	1.00	
Dayton Hudson Co	5331	0	0.98	
Dillbird Dept. Stores	5331	0.04	1.04	
Great At. and Pac. Co	5411	4.68	1.05	
Harcourt General Inc	5311	0.36	1.02	
Kruger Co	5211	0.40	1.03	
Limited Inc	5621	9.48		1.00
Marriott Corp	5812	9.54		1.00
May Dept. Stores	5311	11.90		0.96
McDonalds Corp	5812	0	0.90	
Rite Aid Corp.	5912	1.60	1.07	
Super Value Inc	5140	18.24		1.08
TJX Companies	5651	11.82		1.03
Wal Green Co	5912	1.44	0.93	
Wedy's Inter. Inc	5812	46.84		0.94
Wol-Mart Stores	5331	6.08		0.92
Woolworth Corp	5331	0.10	1.04	

Note: See Table 9.1.

REFERENCES

Bairam, E.I. (1987), *Technical Progress and Industrial Growth, in the USSR and Eastern Europe*, Avebury, Aldershot.

Bairam, E.I. (1991a), Elasticity of Substitution, Technical Progress and Returns to Scale in Branches of Soviet Industry: A New CES Production Function Approach, *Journal of Applied Econometrics*, 6, 91-96.

Bairam, E.I. (1991b), Functional Form and New Production Functions: Some Comments and a New Variable Elasticity of Substitution Function, *Applied Economics*, 23, 1247-1250.

Bairam, E.I. (1994), *Homogeneous and Non-homogeneous Production Functions: Theory and Applications*, Avebury, Aldershot.

Beach, C. and MacKinnon, J. (1978), A Maximum Likelihood Procedure for Regression with Autocorrelated Error, *Econometrica*, 46, 51-58.

Berndt, E.R. and Khaled, M.S. (1979), Parametric Productivity Measurement and Choice Among Flexible Functional Forms, *Journal of Political Economy*, 87 1220-45.

Khaled, M.S. (1979), Choice Among Functional Forms: A Parametric Approach Based on the Generalized Box-Cox Functional Form, Discussion Papers, Department of Economics, University of British Colombia.

Standard and Poor's (1993), *Computstat*, McGraw - Hill, New York.